The Long Road to Easy Street

*A Memoir
In Nineteen Movements*

Margaret Pacsu

Copyright © 2025 by Margaret Pacsu

All rights reserved

No part of this book may be reproduced, stored in a retrieval system, or transmitted by any means, electronic, mechanical, photocopying, recording, or otherwise, without written permission from the author or publisher. There is one exception. Brief passages may be quoted in articles or reviews.

Library and Archives Canada Cataloguing in Publication

CIP data on file with the National Library and Archives

ISBN 978-1-55483-592-8 (trpb)
ISBN 978-1-55483-593-5 (e-book)

Cover design by Laura Boyle

Dedication

To my steadfast and brilliant partner, Bob Campbell, without whom I would never have made it to Easy Street.

And to my two lovely children and their equally lovely partners whose unstinting enthusiasm and support in so many ways was a continuous encouragement.

Acknowledgments

Many people have been generous with their help, particularly:

Dinah Forbes, my splendid editor who has always believed in this undertaking and kept me on the right road.

Jan Tennant, my friend and colleague at CBC who once spent an entire vacation flight from her home in Vancouver to Toronto proofreading my MS. Well done.

Judy Maddren, who always smiled even when CBC management was misbehaving, and was generous in her recollection of our experiences in the old Radio Building.

Mary Lou Creechan, who has stood by me and given me her opinion on the MS, as well as health, politics, men and the distress of growing old. Fortunately, we both like the same wine.

Brian Levine, CEO of the Glenn Gould Foundation, a loyal colleague who has kept me in touch with Glenn's legion of admirers around the world.

Peter O'Brien, an editor and author – most recently of *Love & Let Go* – who freely offered suggestions and insightful advice.

John Miller, former Executive Director of the Glenn Gould Foundation, long-time Director of the Stratford Music Festival, and currently Artistic Director of the annual Huron Waves music festival, recalled dates and events with patience and admirable clarity.

Dan Beach is the young film maker I met at WGBH in 1961. I cherish his photos and his friendship. We have been in touch for the last 64 years, but we remain 22 years old whenever we look at the pictures.

Tony Hillman, an outstanding journalist, was the first person in 1972 to welcome me to CBLT, protect me and encourage me to ignore the old hands who saw me as working in the "sand box" reporting "puff pieces." We have stayed friends over these last 53 years.

Contents

1.	Love Lost	7
2.	What Eleanor Roosevelt didn't hear	31
3.	Assault in Warsaw	46
4.	Tear gassed in Paris	62
5.	Abed with John Cleese	69
6.	Joining the CBC's RAF	83
7.	Bad weather for bunnies	92
8.	Why you shouldn't talk too much to Margaret Atwood	100
9.	"The Kremlin's" goodbye	115
10.	The rinky-dink piano player	120
11.	How to make a house haunted	135
12.	Márta meets Glenn	146
13.	Picnic basket surprise	159
14.	Meeting the ravens	167
15.	The Pope and the baby	172
16.	No love for torch singers at "The Kremlin"	179
17.	The road opens to "Easy Street"	194
18.	Kurt Vonnegut car salesman	210
19.	Love recovered	223

Chapter 1

Love Lost

In Paris, even March can be beautiful, but it wasn't that night in 1963. It was freezing. Icy rain, almost snow, swirled around the grey buildings lining the Rue d'Artois in the chic 8th arrondissement. My umbrella was useless. I was cold, and my feet were wet, but up ahead I could see the warm light of the Blue Note, my destination. It was a supper club, offering dinners and all-night dancing, but was best known as the home of American jazz in Paris. That's why I was headed there. Inside the front door, the walls were hung with dozens of framed photographs of jazz musicians. A few I recognized, among them Duke Ellington and Django Reinhardt, but most of the photos were faded, having hung there for decades. Chet was on the wall too – Chet Baker, wearing a straw hat, sitting on a stool and holding his trumpet upright on his knee. A cigarette was in his other hand, of course. He looked straight back at me with his haunted eyes. It was Chet I had come to see. I could already hear his trio playing the final bars of "My Funny Valentine".

The hallway led to a smallish room with a low ceiling. There were only a dozen or so people seated at small tables around the bandstand – a sparse, rainy Thursday night crowd. Most were young, well dressed, even trendy and drinking colourful cocktails. Chet and his group were dressed in white shirts and grey trousers, a conservative look.

"Bonsoir, mademoiselle. Where would you like to sit?"

"Over there," I said, indicating a table for two in the back corner.

"Are you expecting someone?" he asked.

"I don't know."

Spotlights were focused on the stage, and the rest of the room was dark except for friendly circles of light spilling onto each table from lamps with frilly pink-and-white shades. In front of the bandstand there was a small, polished floor for dancing, and for once there was not a lot of smoke from Gitane and Gauloise cigarettes clouding the air. My Prince of Cool, looking thin and pale, his eyes shut, now concentrating on playing "The Thrill is Gone," I realized he was stoned, but the trio sounded just like they did on my Pacific Jazz LP. I knew the song by heart. I could have sung it with him. I would have too, if he'd seen me in my dark corner and invited me to join him. That's why I had gone to the club. I wanted him to look at me and not from a photo. I was exactly his type: blonde, pretty, a fan. I'd showered with Chanel No. 5 soap earlier that night, and I was wearing a soft, light blue cashmere sweater that suited me to a tee. I didn't know quite what to expect.

Chet and the guys stopped playing. But instead of coming to the back of the room, offering me a drink, putting his arms around me, and telling me how he'd been longing for me to drop by the club, he pulled up a chair on the stage, slumped in it and closed his eyes. The other two parts of the trio headed for the bar.

"Is he going to play again?" I asked a passing waiter.

"Well, mademoiselle, sometimes he does and sometimes he doesn't. It just depends on his mood." And then with a shrug, "They're artists, you know."

I waited for a while, but nothing happened. Chet continued to nod in his chair, a few new customers wandered in, and the group that was there when I arrived paid their bill and left. I reluctantly decided to leave too. Shortly afterward, I read in the *Herald Tribune* that he'd cut short his engagement at the Blue Note and gone to Germany for help with his drug addiction. Another Chet Baker hit, "Let's Get

Lost," made the charts.

I walked home, my feet still wet, leaving footprints in the snow. If anyone had been following me, they wouldn't have seen a wobbly track, but I'd had enough wine to fuel a comfortable melancholia, the kind of pensiveness that passes for insight, and I realized two things. The first was that, despite Chet's laconic musical effort and total failure to recognize, let alone acknowledge my devotion, I still loved jazz. I loved the music and the musicians who made it so special and even the places they played it.

The second was that it wasn't Chet the man who'd drawn me to the Blue Note, it was Chet the jazz player, standing on the stage in the spotlight. I wanted to be with him next to the piano in that smoky spotlight, hearing glasses clink and the murmur of conversation. Maybe I'd even sing a duet with him – that part was a little fuzzy. But I now knew that what I'd most wanted was to be on stage in front of those people. It was the spotlight I craved.

Life in Princeton, New Jersey, in the late 1940s and early 1950s was like an experimental theatre production, covered minutely by both local newspapers, *Town Topics* and *The Princeton Packet*. They provided an endless stream of articles about the town's Nobel Prize winners, the brilliant scientists from eastern Europe and Hungary who had worked on the Manhattan Project. Now, like my father, Eugene Pacsu, they did their research at the university, although the others were physicists, and he was a chemist. The two newspapers also reported on concerts by such notables as Paul Robeson, whose beautiful voice had made him an international celebrity, and on the social events of the rich and famous townies. *Town Topics* also ran stories about debutants, visitors to the yachts of the rich, and the well-known actors who performed at the elegant MacArthur Theatre on their way to New York or between Hollywood films.

Small towns usually have a main drag named Main Street and numbered streets ranked behind it. Not Princeton. Princeton streets are named for the signatories of the Declaration of Independence. Its main street, for example, is named after the American revolutionary Richard Stockton, an interesting choice since he was the only one to sign the nation's founding document and then later sign an oath of allegiance to the British Crown. There is also Witherspoon Street, named after John of the same name, Washington Avenue and, of course, the Lincoln Highway, running from Princeton to Trenton.

The house where I grew up just outside Princeton, New Jersey, was once the gardener's cottage on an estate owned by the United States' wartime ambassador to Britain. Just behind it is the edge of the Magic Woods where my sister and I played.

Winant Road, where I grew up, is named after John Gilbert Winant, another high achiever, although of rather dubious character. A romantic figure, he became the first man to win three terms as Republican governor of New Hampshire, then, thanks to President Roosevelt, became American ambassador to Great Britain throughout the Second World War. It wasn't an entirely dark time for him. He had a rather public affair with Winston Churchill's louche daughter Sarah, much to the chagrin of his wife, Constance Rivington Russell, back in

Princeton. She had inherited the 273-acre Edgerstoune property from her father, Archibald Russell. It was eventually subdivided, and my parents bought the gardener's cottage situated on a beautiful parcel of land we called the Magic Wood. When Mr. Winant returned home in 1947, learned that his wife was divorcing him and that he was heavily in debt, he shot and killed himself. Churchill sent four dozen roses. The King and Queen sent condolences. There is a hit musical movie from 1951 I have always liked called "Royal Wedding." Sarah Churchill has a major role in it, dancing with Fred Astaire – something I have always dreamed of doing. I always wondered if Mr. Winant could keep up with her on the dance floor.

The town's most famous citizen, Albert Einstein, was frequently in the press. Sometimes the story was about his unusual point of view on a new political matter. I never met him, but I often saw him walking near his house on Mercer Street. He was known to talk with his neighbors about up-coming concerts, his love for Mozart, his cherished violin and piano. He spoke with their teenaged children about math and algebra, although these conversations didn't improve my classmates' marks. They would make it into the local papers, though, because anything to do with Professor Einstein made headlines. On April 18, 1955, at 8:30 a.m. I was pushing a cart containing magazines, newspapers, candy bars and fruit juice around the hallways of the Princeton Hospital, fulfilling the requirement to do social service before graduating from high school, when a nurse told us that Dr. Einstein had died at 1:15 a.m. that morning.

Einstein had been vice-president of the Princeton Symphony Orchestra between 1927 and 1955. It mounted a concert in his memory, led by the Hungarian-born conductor Nicholas Harsányi, the following December. My mother, Márta, a classical pianist also from Hungary, performed, as did about every classical musician in the area. She knew Einstein as a violinist and thought that, although he did not play at a professional standard, his great love of music always came through. Renowned French concert pianist Robert Casadesus, who stayed with his family in Princeton during the Second World War, played the "Coronation Concerto, Homage to the King," by Mozart, written in 1790.

During and after the war, the Institute of Advanced Study in Princeton attracted many great scholars, including, in 1947, Robert Oppenheimer, who was its director until 1966. Before joining the institute, he was involved in the Manhattan Project along with the Hungarian physicists Edward Teller, Eugene Wigner and mathematician John von Neumann, whose daughter Marina was in my sister's class.

Living in the same town as all those famous people should have been inspiring, but it was not for me. Their accomplishments represented closed doors. Why try anything when they'd already done it, and a lot better than I probably could? Besides I didn't want to be a physicist working alone in a laboratory, as my father had, and I imagined physicists did also.

I was lonely growing up amid the greenery of the Magic Wood on Winant Road. My parents had arrived in Princeton from Hungary in 1930 after my father was offered the position of assistant professor of organic carbohydrate chemistry at the university. Earlier, my father's brilliance in chemistry had come to the attention of the American government, and he had worked for two years in Washington at the Bureau of Standards. My mother had come with him and had even played a well-received concert while there. She knew that moving permanently to the States would mean starting her musical career all over again, but she was willing to do that. Princeton promised them both what they could never have had in Hungary: security, money, and the respect given intellectuals. They were welcomed and quickly became a part of the community centred around the university.

Four years later, my father was promoted to associate professor, and they bought the small house on Winant Road. It was two miles from the centre of Princeton and Dad's office, but my mother could practice piano there without restraint. There were no neighbours close enough to hear. It was a magical place. There were no children nearby either, as ours was the only house on the road in those days.

Summer of 1944. My sister Anne (on the left) and I at home after splashing in the garden hose .

My sister, Anne, was born in Princeton in 1934 and I arrived four years later on June 27, 1938. Our age difference meant we rarely played together, especially after she started going to school. I was left to my own devices, and on warm days I explored the field opposite our house. In early summer it was filled with sweet, small wild strawberries, violets, and intricate Queen Anne's lace flowers, which I would weave into a crown. Later in the year there were daisies, phlox, and asters. It wasn't all sugar and cream, though. There was also stinging nettle, poison ivy, angry wasps – the storied kind with the impossibly thin waists – and little black ticks.

My mother knew all about ticks. She examined my hair every night, parting it with a kitchen fork, and exclaimed whenever she found one buried in my scalp. There are recommended ways to remove them – a certain kind of tweezers, end of a hot match – but she just dug them out with her fingernails and squeezed them until her fingertips were red with blood. It didn't hurt me much, but it did scare me. We also found them hidden in my socks around my ankles. At the end of this ritual, my mother lined up their red-and-black remains on the kitchen table. I would have been happy to scoop their crushed bodies into the garbage, but she insisted we flush them down the toilet. She thought that was safer.

Winant Road, in those days a gravel road, wasn't well travelled, but there was enough traffic each year to turn it into a washboard. Every summer, a township works crew came by to grade it, then coat it with gravel and spray it with hot tar, which smoothed out the washboard. I loved the tar. It bubbled up in the sun, hot, glossy, and sinuous, and flowed in rivulets across the shoulder. I used a stick to divert the sticky streams and poke at bubbles until they burst, releasing a sharp, wonderful smell. "The King of Tar, the King of Tar," I'd sing in a loud voice as I danced and twirled down the shoulder, careful not to step on the road. But there was never anybody around to hear me or see my clever dance steps.

Just down the road was an odd place we called the smoke house for no known reason. Honeysuckle grew on the sides of the road at that point, and I would stop to suck the nectar out of the blossoms. The smoke house was underground, covered in grass and almost invisible from the road. I'd step down through the vines covering the opening into a chilly cavern that still smelled of smoke. It was a large room, its floor a mixture of pebbles and rubble and broken glass. There were no windows but the remains of a bonfire near the back wall were just visible. I'd shout as loud as I could to hear the echo. I made noises and sang. It was strange and exhilarating to hear my voice bounce back at me. It was almost as if there was another person singing with me or maybe watching me from the dark corner. And then I'd get the shivers and quickly scramble out into the warm sunlight and hurry home. I never told my mother about my visits to the smokehouse or anyone else for that matter. If I'd told, I would have been banned from going back.

Stony Brook ran through the Magic Woods behind our house and was the source of hours of pleasure and discovery. (Photo courtesy of Anne Pacsu)

A tree-covered hill sloped from the lawn at the back of our house down to a creek called Stony Brook. This was the Magic Wood. It was a beautiful place, with unusual flowering trees and edged with dogwoods and lilacs. In the spring, the ground was crowded with purple violets and Mayapples. One sycamore was so big and so old I could walk inside it. It was quiet in there, except for the wind soughing in the branches and the cheerful singing of the brook. An owl lived in the tree, and deer would come to drink from the stream. I waded in the rivulets in the summer when the brook was just trickling along. In the fall when the rains came, it became a fast-running river, overflowing its banks so far that, when the sun shone again, the glittering ripples were reflected on the walls of the kitchen.

A tall pine tree at the edge of the woods kept the ground under it free from other plants and I used the space as an outdoor room. I swept the leaves and twigs away until the dirt was even and clean and dug a layer of bricks in around it so everyone could see the border of my property. Then I invited a prince and princess to come for tea. Sometimes Jacky the Cat – that was his real name – would join us to listen to my stories. And if we were all quiet and well-behaved, which we always were, the white owl that lived in the sycamore would fly over to listen and nod in the branch above us. I was pleased to have such elegant if imaginary friends. What I took so much for granted I barely registered it was the music in the background as my mother practised on her piano.

My mother, who had played the piano since the age of nine, had studied at the famous Conservatory of Music in Budapest with such teachers as Béla Bartók and Zoltán Kodály. She made her debut concert at the age of twenty-three on February 17, 1926, to excellent reviews. Her repertoire consisted of the kind of music she would play the rest of her life: Bach, Mozart, Beethoven, and of course Bartók, who was emerging as a major Hungarian composer. The internationally known French pianist Jeanne-Marie Darré played a solo concert in Budapest at the same time, which diminished the audience for my mother's performance. Nevertheless, it was well received.

My father, Eugene Pacsu, in his chemistry laboratory at Princeton University about 1945. He loved American cigarettes, Lucky Strikes in particular, but stopped smoking them on his doctor's advice from one day to the next soon after this photo was taken. His last half-empty package of cigarettes was still in the top drawer of his desk years afterward.

One day in 1934, shortly after my parents bought the house on Winant Road, my mother went shopping in New York. She came home and told my father that she had bought a 1926 Steinway that would be delivered in two days. My father loved music and so he said nothing. That beautiful instrument remained with my mother for sixty-four years. She practised every day. Dad never practiced but he would play melodies from the 1906 Hungarian operetta "János Vitéz" ("Johnny Corn"). Mum always said that, although she was the professional pianist, it was he who had the talent.

My mother's piano meant there was always music in our household. My sister learned to read music well. I couldn't deal with the timing – no quarter notes, or eighth notes for me. My father was asked to play and sing by my mother's friends and sometimes by his colleagues when he was away at a chemistry conference. He had a warm, friendly voice and I tried to sound like him. My sister and I both have perfect pitch, which means we can sing the sound of an

"A" like a tuning fork. Over the years I have learned to read vocal music but never well enough to accompany myself. I could never figure out the coordination.

Socializing was easy for my father because of his job at the university, where he quickly came to know the other chemists and their associates, students, and other faculty members. Making friends was more difficult for my mother. She looked for people who suited her musically and politically. As an American citizen she voted for little-known socialist Norman Thomas in his futile runs for the presidency. There was one incident around 1936 that my mother liked to relate. She wasn't one to tell jokes or funny stories, but this story always made us laugh.

It was customary for the wives of the chemistry department to invite their husbands' wives to tea, and eventually it was my mother's turn. Sir Hugh Taylor, the Englishman who was chair of the chemistry department, had offered Dad the position at Princeton, and so my mother invited his wife, Lady Elizabeth Taylor, along with the other chemistry wives. It was in the fall, and Mum laid out all kinds of pastries on the dining room table. She had also arranged a beautiful bouquet of bright red fall leaves. They were shiny and the perfect decoration for the centrepiece. The guests enjoyed the tea and pastries, but at one point Lady Taylor came up to my mother and said, "Márta, do you know what those leaves are?" My mother said in her perfect English "No, but they are very pretty," and Lady Taylor said, "Well, my dear, that's what we here call poison ivy. The shiny oil on the leaves gives many people rashes. So that is not something to have on your dining room table as a decoration. You must be careful not to touch them." My mother must have worn gloves to pick and arrange the leaves because she didn't break out in a rash at that time. She did later, whenever my sister and I touched it while playing in the forest or Jacky the Cat would brush against it and then rub on our ankles. But she took Lady Taylor's advice and never picked poison ivy again.

One summer day in 1942, when I was four and Anne was eight, we set off in our green Ford for Point Pleasant on the New Jersey seashore. My parents had saved up enough war time ration points to buy the gas and it wasn't a long trip anyway. They packed a picnic lunch, a thermos of water and a change of clothes in the trunk. We found a spot on the beach that suited everyone and then ran down to the water. My sister could swim, but I only splashed around. After a while our parents called us for lunch, and then we saw that black sticky stuff was covering our legs and bathing suits. My parents had it all over their feet. It wouldn't come off, even though we rubbed and scrubbed. I cried because I was sure my feet and legs would stay black and sticky forever. Dad said it was tar. He said he'd heard rumours that German submarines, U-boats, had torpedoed American oil tankers off the New Jersey coast. Many ships had been attacked within a few miles of the beach. Black oil, oil balls, and wreckage had washed up on the shoreline. In the car going home, we sat on towels. Our parents assured us the tar would come off with turpentine. It did, but we smelled very strange and had to throw our bathing suits out.

My sister and I went in different directions at an early age. She was interested in the sciences, especially in bugs, beetles, and other multi-legged things, and ignored the social pressure of her peers at Miss Fine's School, the girl's day school in Princeton we both attended. I was there for thirteen years and loved it. May Margaret Fine had founded the school at the turn of the twentieth century, and the standards there were still very high, which appealed to Princeton academics. Shirley Davis became headmistress in September 1943, the year I entered kindergarten, and watched over me for many years. My mother became the school's music assistant. I found out later, she never received a salary: her work paid my tuition. Many of my classmates came from very wealthy families. I did not. This occasionally caused discord. However, there were opportunities for me there that hinted at my future interests – plays, musical groups, dances, and later, dates with the undergraduates from Princeton University.

My mother, Márta Pacsu, in an evening gown before leaving home to give a performance. About 1939. She performed in Washington and New York and regularly in the Princeton area where she also taught piano. She was a beautiful woman who enjoyed performing as much as she enjoyed the opportunity it offered to wear elegant gowns.

My mother gave concerts at various venues in Princeton and at university events, and for many years she taught children every day after school. We would come home to find the living room door closed, which signalled that a student was with my mother. I often took advantage of this to head to the closet where Mum kept her beautiful concert gowns. It was a magical refuge, and dress-up was one of my favorite activities. I'd slip into one of her dresses, perhaps the deep purple chiffon one, a pair of silver shoes made of a stretchy material, which fit the best, and one of her hats with a veil, like the movie stars wore. Then I'd present myself to my imaginary audience and sometimes also Jacky the Cat and admire my shimmering self in a full-length mirror. I would curtsey and twirl around to make sure the back row had a good look at my golden hair.

I had some opportunities at an early age to stand in front of a real audience too, and one year I was the Angel Gabriel in our Sunday school's Christmas pageant. It was a dream come true for this nine-year-old girl, who loved the attention the stage brought. My mother made me a flowing white robe from a bedsheet, golden wings constructed on wire hangers and a handsome golden halo.

I looked forward to it for weeks, but two days before the performance my stomach started to roil. How was I going manage in my clean white angel costume when I was spending most of my time in the bathroom?

Princeton's Trinity Church is large, my classmates would be there, their parents with them and even some teachers. The church had been decorated for days with evergreen boughs, ribbons and Christmas wreaths attached to every other pew. Candles and bright red poinsettias surrounded the altar. The church was ready, I wasn't. I made it through the dress rehearsal, but barely, darting down the hall to the bathroom, leaving all the little angels waiting for me. The performance was the next day, and by now I was dreading it.

"But what if I feel sick?" I asked my mother. "I won't be able to slip out, everyone will notice." My mother felt my forehead and said

I should stay home and in bed. "No! I won't. I'm not sick. I'm going to do it," I said, heading back to the bathroom. I was going to be the angel. By 4:00 p.m., showtime, snow was falling, the church was full, and the organist was playing familiar Christmas carols. My mother was in a front-row pew looking worried. I was scared and my stomach rumbled. Then the music started, and the director pointed at me. I stepped in front of the altar and a dozen shepherds and little angels and picked up the microphone. My voice was strong and filled the church as I recited the message of the birth of Christ. "The angel said unto them, 'Fear not, for behold, I bring you good tidings of great joy which shall be unto all people.'" At the end of the familiar words, the cherubim surrounded me with adoration in their eyes, the shepherds bowed, and we all took the long walk from the altar to the church door. The audience applauded.

"It was wonderful, Margy darling," my mother said afterward. She was relieved, but not nearly as much as I was. I'd made it and without incident. It was my first turn on a stage, and I was hooked. I only wished it had lasted longer.

More theatrical roles followed. When I was in sixth grade, my class put on a play in French for the entire school. Called *L'oiseau bleu*, *The Bluebird of Happiness*, it was written by Maurice Maeterlinck, perhaps his most famous work, and directed by our teacher, who was Russian but spoke beautiful French. There were several roles, but the principal ones were the brother and sister who search for the Bluebird and the good fairy who looks after them. She first appears as a crone but turns into a charming young spirit and sets the plot in motion. I tried out for all three main characters, but the greatest challenge is to turn from an old woman into the good fairy. That's the part I wanted. After several rehearsals, the teacher agreed to cast me. The role was mine. It took considerable effort to make sure my French was correct and to memorize the lengthy script. Changing my costume and personality in front of the audience took additional practise.

Rehearsals went well, but when I walked into the classroom the day before our performance, the teacher looked at me and burst into tears.

"Tes cheveux, tu t'es coupé les cheveux," she said, wiping her eyes.

"Oui," I said. "It's a new haircut, madame, for our play. I didn't want to wear braids as the good fairy. They were too childish. I thought a grown-up style would look more appropriate. I thought you would like it."

"Oh, mon enfant, I imagined you could transform yourself instantly on stage just by removing the black cloak. Voilà, the audience would see the good fairy with all your beautiful blonde hair falling over your shoulders. I made you a black satin and diamond hair band to hold your hair in place like a crown."

"Oh madame, I didn't realize that was why you gave me this part."

"Non, non, mon enfant, you will be the good fairy and as long as you've saved your braids, we can just add some of the old hair to the satin band."

My old hair. I felt discouraged. I can be so reckless and rush into situations without foreseeing the consequences. But the new hair style did look becoming, and we had to give a second performance for all the students. I put my braids in a little cedar box just in case – I didn't know what for. I still have them.

My parents decided to send me to a girl's camp on the shores of Lake Wentworth in New Hampshire for the summers of 1952 and 1953. My sister had gone there one summer but it wasn't a success. The girls called her "nature girl," and not in a kind way, because she was mostly interested in insects and plants, and Valley Camp specialized in dance and drama, my interests. The drama program was rigorous, and I learned more about acting, improvisation and stage management there than anywhere else in my life. My dance skills were poor, but I did well as a narrator for the various ballet story lines. The two women who ran the camp, Etta Johnson and Marlys "Bee" Bach, had a goal: to teach us independence and self-confidence. We had daily classes in acting and evenings of improvised comedy. The guests at a nearby lodge were an eager audience for our major productions as well as the ad lib work. They always applauded loudly, which I thought was the best part. The principal play the first summer I was there was *The Lamp and the Bell*, a complicated drama by Edna St. Vincent Millay. The leading roles were two sisters, I tried out for one of them and got the part. Some of the other campers were upset that a newcomer was chosen, but others felt it was about time. I was just happy to have such a chance. The principal ballet of the summer was based on Lewis Carroll's *Through the Looking-Glass*. It was a pleasure to be the narrator as there were funny voices to do and I didn't have to dance.

I liked Valley Camp. The surroundings were beautiful, and I even learned to canoe. The only problem I had that first summer was that I couldn't swim. For years, I had hidden my fear of water, holding onto the edge at pool parties and refusing classmates' invitations to get-togethers if swimming would be part of the entertainment. However, at Valley Camp being able to swim was a rule. Etta and Bee were required to hire a certified Red Cross instructor. My fellow campers knew I was afraid of water, and one day someone declared there would be no lunch until Margy jumped off the dock. All fifty girls lined up to watch me jump in and started shouting, "We want lunch, we want lunch." I closed my eyes and jumped. Miracle of miracles, I kicked to the surface and kicked again to keep floating. A cheer went up and we all went inside to eat. Never an Olympian, but at least I could stop myself from sinking. I can still hear those shouts of approval and applause

During my second summer, 1953, we put on a creepy Victorian crime drama written by two English authors in the late 1930s titled

Ladies in Retirement. In 1941, a movie version, with Ida Lupino, Elsa Lanchester, and Louis Hayward, had great success.

I played Ellen, one of the two dotty ladies – what the English call the amiably eccentric. Miss Fisk is sitting by the fire reading one evening when I creep up behind her and strangle her with the belt from her new robe. I then drag her into the kitchen and stuff her into the partially open, old bricked-up oven. A delightful plot! Ellen, the murderer, is still my most favorite role ever. Playing her required lots of physical action, dealing with the eccentric roles of my fellow actors, and wearing period costumes. The guests in the lodge, our faithful audience next door to the camp, requested another performance the following evening. We obliged. The success of *Ladies in Retirement* gave me the confidence to try out for some of the major plays at Miss Fine's School.

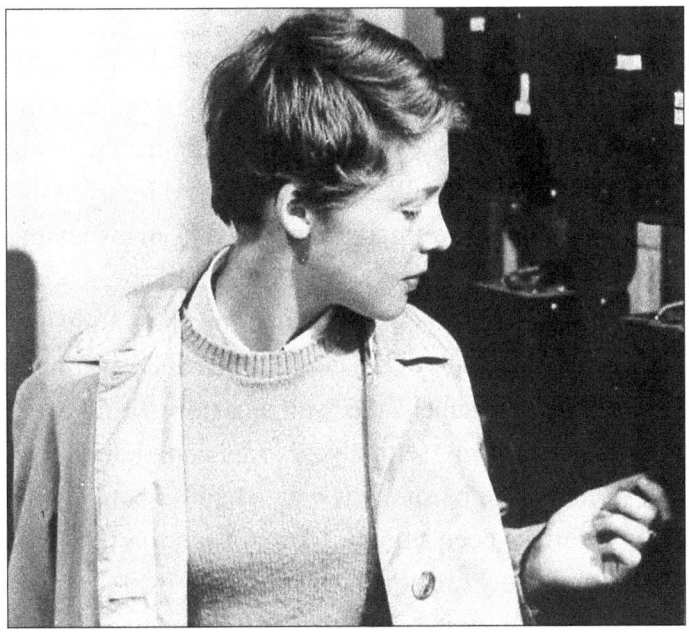

I loved all aspects of the theatre, even the theatre classes at Miss Fine's School, although I'm not sure how genuine my interest is in the school's new electrical panel which appears to have captured my interest here. About 1955. (Photo courtesy of Jack Henderson)

During my four high school years at Miss Fine's, we had a professional director, Roe Wade, for our major plays. Boys from Princeton University joined the cast, and we presented large-scale productions. My senior year I was elected president of the drama club although I had no idea who voted for me or why. I had leading roles and enjoyed playing romantic parts. Our grade nine play, Peter Green's large-scale *The Lost Colony*, which is always performed outdoors, is a true tale about a group of English settlers in sixteenth-century Virginia who all disappeared within three years. I had the role of Governor John White's daughter Eleanor Dare, who might be considered a feminist in today's world. She tries to organize the women and children to save them. The school photo of the last scene depicts Eleanor leading a final prayer session, surrounded by her community, not unlike the Angel Gabriel declaiming to shepherds and cherubs.

In 1956, my senior year, we (together with the Princeton boys) performed *The Enchanted* by the French playwright Jean Giraudoux. His outlook is profoundly cynical, and the themes he explores are society's absurdity and people's lust for money. I played the part of Isabel, a schoolteacher in a small town who falls in love with a ghost. He infects her class with whimsy. There is a murder. A rescue mission keeps Isabel from the hands of death, and the ghost vanishes. We all loved the play. Roe Wade got the best performance ever out of all us teenagers. My role as Isabel fit as well as a new spring coat.

One production, in my senior year, was completely unlike anything I've done before or since. It was an ad lib comedy about our classmates. We had been together from kindergarten to our final grade twelve and knew each other's faults and positive qualities. The girls insisted I be the emcee of this bizarre show made up of spontaneous comments about and by my classmates. I wore an "improv" kind of outfit: dark glasses, a big straw hat, shorts and high heels and pranced across the stage with my microphone, interviewing my classmates. The audience began to laugh, and the longer I wandered around the stage, the louder the laughter at our foolish remarks was. It worked, but I found it a difficult kind of performance, so it was my first and last improvised comedy show.

Over the years, the head mistress, Shirley Davis, and Mrs. Shepherd, head of the senior English class and editor of our yearbook, had seen all my work on stage. One day Miss Davis called me into her office, which usually was never a good sign. So I was surprised when she said, "Margy, Mrs. Shepherd and I would like to enter you in a poetry-reading contest. You will be representing Miss Fine's School at the eighteenth annual all-state event for New Jersey secondary schools in the reading of poetry, presented by Rutgers College. Would you like to do this?" Not much choice there. "Mrs. Shepherd will drive you there and stay with you." Of course, I said yes.

> # Margaret Pacsu
>
> will represent this school at the eighteenth annual all-state contest for New Jersey secondary schools in the Reading of Poetry
> March 3, 1956
>
> Arts and Sciences
> The Newark College of **RUTGERS** of Rutgers University
> in
> **NEWARK**
> THE STATE UNIVERSITY
> OF NEW JERSEY
> 18 Washington Place, Newark

New Jersey's Rutgers University held a poetry reading contest in the spring of 1956 and Miss Fine's School sent me to represent the school. Of 30 student poetry readers, I was one of the two finalists. The winner read a story not a poem, a perceived unfairness that rankled.

So, on March 3, 1956, we drove to Newark and found our way to a cavernous, chilly, and poorly lit auditorium. There were some thirty or more contestants representing public and private schools from all over New Jersey and a scattering of parents and friends. We sat quietly for a couple of hours in this strange atmosphere while three judges ran the auditions. All our young voices echoed in the mostly empty space. After they had eliminated all the other contestants, it came down to two of us: me and another girl. She read her piece in an outrageously melodramatic and loud voice, her arms flapping like towels on a clothesline. It was prose, no doubt about it, it was not poetry.

When my turn came, I read my modest poem by Robert Frost clearly but quietly, hands at my sides, then hurried back to my seat. Mrs. Shephard gave me an encouraging smile. The winner was announced. The other girl won first prize, and Robert Frost and I received an honorable mention. Mrs. Shephard and I knew the girl had not read a poem in verse and were both puzzled why the judges had placed her first, but it was New Jersey. I still have the certificate from Rutgers, though, with my name embossed in gold. Miss Davis was very pleased to have Miss Fine's School listed among the winners, and I was delighted to have my name on such a fine-looking document, although privately I felt slightly cheated.

On a Tuesday evening in June, the class of 1956 graduated from Miss Fine's School. It was a wonderful evening. After choral music and speeches, the academic awards were presented. My marks had never been brilliant but, aside from math, I'd managed to keep up. To my astonishment and pleasure at last I made the academic honor roll after years of just missing it. In the official photo of award winners, we are wearing white dresses and holding huge bouquets of red roses. We look young, beautiful, and ready for whatever life will bring us. The music played, the guests and parents applauded, and we left. Despite shifting loyalties and competition in the past, I felt close to my classmates and the quaint old inn that served as our school.

In the "Best Known For" section of our 1956 yearbook its brilliant editor, Grace Morton, wrote that I was the most "effervescent"; my besetting sin was "being mercurial"; my saving grace "spontaneity"; my *Bête Noire* "the Old Country"; I was most likely to "start a Socialist uprising" (wouldn't Mum be proud); and my favorite song was "The Lady is a Tramp."

Mostly true!

Chapter 2

What Eleanor Roosevelt didn't hear

In late autumn 1956, I was living deep in western Massachusetts, alone, and homesick. I had made a mistake and didn't know how to fix it. My mother had suggested I go to Radcliffe College in Boston where, she said, there were many cultural organizations and the chance for me to meet intelligent young men at Harvard and other institutions. I refused, telling her I had had enough of young men buzzing around me in Princeton. It was true. I was pretty and easy to talk to. The boys all wanted to take me out for cozy walks and much more, but it was the early 1950s, and first base was far enough. I said I wanted to go to Smith College in rural Massachusetts. The discussion, which my father wisely stayed out of, went back and forth for days. In the end, I won, not that I was more persuasive or had a better argument, but because my mother stopped talking about it. All my classmates did well on the Scholastic Aptitude Test and were accepted at the colleges of their choice. The Smith Club in Princeton even gave me a small scholarship.

It wasn't until after I arrived at Smith I learned we were allowed only six weekends a year off campus for a visit home, and those only if your marks were good enough. That's the rule, they said, no exceptions. There were hundreds of girls in my class, not the twenty of us in the class of 1956 at Miss Fine's School. Many of the students were smart and very rich and had attended renown prep schools. A few of them even had cars hidden away in Northampton, the local town.

At first, I buried myself in schoolwork and activities and even managed to get elected president of one of the two freshman choirs. I took this to be something of an honour until I found out the job was mainly sorting through music, arranging risers, and selling tickets. Still, the choir did sound beautiful, and we sang with choirs from our neighboring universities, Yale and Amhurst. I loved singing and I was proud of this choir, but as holding office was leading nowhere, I resigned after Christmas.

Although Smith's western Massachusetts location was beautiful and many of its courses were compelling, I was dismayed at being tucked away in Northampton. It just wasn't a good fit. So I applied to transfer to another college, Radcliffe or Columbia. An admissions officer at Radcliffe told me they accepted only three transfer students a year. Columbia said they would admit me as a French major, but I would have to take Romanian for a year as a Latin-based language like French. Romanian! I was raised to be a Hungarian at heart and really did not want to take Romanian.

I was lucky. I often am. Whenever I reach a brick wall and run out of ideas, something always comes up. Pierce Mulholland, an old friend from Princeton, drove from Connecticut one afternoon along with five of his college roommates. They had bought an old hearse seemingly as long as a city block, which they had christened the Queen Mary, and took me and some others for rides through the countryside. I told him about wanting to transfer and my frustration at not finding the right college to go to. Pierce, who was a smart guy and a wonderful painter, shrugged and said, "Forget another school. Go to Paris."

"What do you mean? Quit Smith?"

"Nah. Go to Paris on a Smith College Junior Year Abroad program. You will love Paris. I love Paris. Every painter loves Paris. It will change your life." When I talked to my parents about it, amazingly they thought it was a wonderful idea. Problem possibly solved.

I was one of forty-two girls enrolled in the 1958 Smith program in Paris. The weather during our transatlantic trip in early September on the SS *Flandre* from New York to Le Havre was calm, and we spent our first six weeks in Aix-en-Provence "adapting," as the school put it, to life in France. There was a lot to adapt to: the language, the food – especially the many cheeses and wines – the narrow streets of the ancient villages, and the stunning landscape have plunged us into another world. The six weeks went by fast and then we were taken back to Paris and moved in with the French families who were accommodating us for the next year. I was placed with Mme Robert de Renty, who had worked with the Free French during the Second World War and wore her Legion d'Honneur proudly. She was a real countess, and her daughter had gone to Mt. Holyoke College in the late 1940s, so she felt comfortable boarding young American women from similarly privileged backgrounds. For the 1949-50 academic year, her young lodger was none other than Jacqueline Bouvier, and they had remained in touch. Madame and I also forged a modest international *amitié*.

Drinking champagne at Reid Hall in Paris, 1959. It wasn't my first taste of wine of course, but it was likely my first taste of real champagne. I loved Paris and our classes. I made friends there that would change my life.

It took me a while to find my way around the city and to settle into the college schedule at Reid Hall, the Parisian campus for several American colleges. The academic work was not too challenging, and I spent many evenings listening to the radio, beginning to explore a whole new world of beautiful sounds – at first, older artists like Charles Trenet, Edith Piaf, and even Josephine Baker. I found a small "cave" near the Seine at the end of boulevard Saint Michel that played nothing but American jazz as background music.

Pierce was right, I loved Paris. Everything was a new, exciting experience. There was just one problem: money. I still had some scholarship funds, but it was not enough, not in Paris. Did I really need more? No, probably not. My room and board and all medical expenses were covered. But how could any young woman walking by Dior's window not stop to admire those elegant plain black high heel shoes and not really, really, badly want them?

One weekend, the Smith administrators at Reid Hall organized a tea dance with some of the other American colleges. There I met a quiet young man from Niagara Falls, New York, who was studying to be a lawyer and like me, was on a tight budget. I told him about my interest in drama and music, and he told me about his freelance work for the French national broadcaster (ORTF). Would I be interested? The pay would be modest, around ten dollars a session.

We went there the next day. I read part of a script, and they hired me. Just like that. They knew I had never done radio recordings before, but it didn't seem to matter. The staff at the station gave me good advice about voice production, pitch, and clarity. The job didn't pay much, but the programs, all in English about French history, were broadcast on WNYC in New York. This meant that my parents could listen to them. I got ten dollars a program, but I should have paid these people for the experience.

After my academic year in Paris, I returned to Smith College and graduated the following year with a degree in French and history. I spent that summer in New York with Charlotte, my best friend from Miss Fine's School, studying speedwriting, a kind of shorthand, and typing. I did all right with the typing, but I flunked the speedwriting course. I took this to be nature's way of telling me to stay away from secretarial work, the most common job for women in those days.

The Smith vocational office helped me get a job at the Center for Middle Eastern Studies at Harvard University, where I met a young Syrian man. He was a member of the Church of Antioch, born in Brooklyn, and he fascinated me. We got engaged – that involved a ring, monogrammed towels, a wedding dress, silverware, and my putting up with his calling me his "little rabbit." That wasn't all of course, and the closer we got – and the closer the wedding day got – the more I intuited that marrying him was not a good idea. The prospect of the marriage ritual and commitment made me feel as if I were drowning, wrapped up in yards of stifling lace. I would be a housewife, a little rabbit in some bland suburb, and inevitably washed away. I was scared stiff when I did it, but six weeks before the wedding I said no, I'm not going through with it. In response, he wrote me tender, affectionate letters, and I still have this note: "Spring here is, but slowly and precisely, and of a green that hurts. And though the German Jew tells us that from the great hurt came the little songs, I ask how a man sings, who knows she measures her wellbeing in terms of undoing her love?"

I was in an emotional turmoil. One winter day I drove out to a deserted beach in Gloucester. I walked down to the water's edge and kept going. The waves were crashing around me higher and higher, and I was shivering and soaking wet. I had no idea what I was doing, standing waist-deep in the swirling water, but the noise of the wind and the gulls brought me to my senses before I went any deeper. It was clear something dangerous was about to happen. I stumbled back to the car and drove home. I was already seeing a psychiatrist – Betsy, my boss, had given me his name. I told him what I had done, and he took it seriously. So did I. We never did discover the root of my anxiety and fear – that came much later – but Dr. Miles helped me to get through many difficult months.

I quit my job and forgot speedwriting as quickly as I could and resolved never to be anyone's little rabbit. But resolve only carries you so far. I did nothing but go to movies, listen to my jazz collection, and moon over my French records. I needed a job, but the only ones advertised were for secretaries or salesgirls.

Then I saw the ad that changed my life. WGBH-TV in Boston was looking for an aide to the assistant manager, sort of an assistant to the assistant, the interviewer told me. He hired me after he heard I'd worked in broadcasting, even though that was in radio. WGBH-TV was the first publicly funded TV station in New England, broadcasting, it said, programs about "intellectual subjects." It was a small, three-camera operation that could handle both live and taped broadcasts.

My role was to help my boss, Dave Davis, who, among other

things, directed a season of six live TV concerts by the Boston Symphony Orchestra, conducted by Charles Munch. "It'll be fun," he said. "You'll be in the control room with me."

The control room turned out to be a mobile one, parked outside the concert hall on the street. It was an old Greyhound bus—one of those now iconic, streamlined, round-backed buses – with the windows painted over. When we got there, he handed me a pile of musical scores. "These are yours," he said, bouncing up the several steps into the bus ahead of me. I followed. My job was to read the score two measures ahead of the music and warn Dave, who was directing the five cameramen and the switcher, what section of the orchestra would be playing next. He cued the camera to stand by, and when the string section was about to start told the switcher to "Take four" and then "Take two" and so on. I could read music well enough to keep two measures ahead of the orchestra, although a two-hour live concert with four of us and our equipment jammed together in a hot and smelly old bus was exhausting. I had never imagined there even was such a job, let alone that I could do it, but it was exciting, and it was in television, which was still a new technology. I felt like a valuable part of a team when we ended on the same note at the finale.

I met all the producers at the station, there were about ten of them (only two were women), the lighting and set design people, the managers and, of course, the secretaries (all of them women). The studio was in a shabby building, an old skating rink, and had little of the glamour associated with television, but we were all aware that working in non-commercial television was a privilege. We didn't have to peddle dish soap or coffee or walking aids.

One young producer, Dan Beach, was seriously influenced by movie actor and director John Cassavetes, known at the time for *Shadows*, an innovative film about three weeks in the lives of three brothers, two of whom are struggling jazz musicians. It was said to have been completely improvisational and shot without a script, a significant innovation. That turned out not to be the case, but not before it influenced a legion of filmmakers, including Dan.

He said he was shooting the same kind of unrehearsed film and asked me if I would be in it. Would I be his "girl on the Ferris wheel?" You bet I would. I accepted instantly and we got to work. The short film was shot entirely while we were whirling around on the carnival ride. Despite the title, I hadn't realized that my feet wouldn't touch the ground for hours, leaving my introduction to film acting vaguely nausea inducing. It may not have been Oscar-worthy, but it was a professional piece of work. And an exhilarating experience for me. Margy in the movies at last. I hoped that next time I'd be able to keep my feet on the ground.

I went home to Princeton for the weekend on Saturday, October 14, 1961, with much to tell my parents about the Boston Symphony concerts, my little film, and the generally cheerful atmosphere of the station. I was happy, and they were very happy for me. Then on Sunday morning, Dave, my boss, called me from Boston. "Might as well stay in Princeton," he said. "The station has burned down." On Friday night, he explained, the WGBH building had caught fire, and little remained but ashes, twisted metal, and a few smoldering beams.

I took the first train back to Boston and joined my colleagues as they trampled through the charred rubble. Everyone was trying to save equipment, films, precious tapes, but most of it had been destroyed or damaged beyond repair. It was heartbreaking. Management moved quickly. Within one day, WGBH-TV started broadcasting mainly out of the Newman Catholic Center. His Eminence Cardinal Richard Cushing supported the modest station and called on local universities to pitch in and help restore all its programming. It wasn't help without strings, though. There were conditions – certain topics were off limits. Birth control was one, a lively subject in 1961, just months after the FDA had approved the revolutionary birth control pill that would change women's lives. With the prospect of enough funding to stay on the air, management quickly agreed that we wouldn't mention birth control or abortion – another hotly debated subject even ten years before Roe v. Wade. The station raised a million dollars in the first week after the fire.

Among the first programs broadcast on the resurrected WGBH was "Jazz with Father O'Connor." I loved everything about jazz, from the personalities of its musicians to its current popular form, bebop. I especially loved the modern, cool sound. When I still lived at home in Princeton, university students would drive some of us Miss Fine's School girls into New York on the weekends to go to jazz clubs. The boys at eighteen were old enough to get into places like Birdland, where Charlie Parker was a headliner. But we girls were too young. We stood on the sidewalk to listen to him play. Only the Metropole at 7th Avenue and 48th Street welcomed us at age sixteen. The bartenders there, almost certainly with limited vision, never asked for identification and served us as much beer as we could drink.

I had two jazz teachers. Radio DJ Al "Jazzbo" Collins was my first coach, instructor, and inspiration about all things jazz when I was barely a teenager. He broadcast every evening from ten to midnight on WNEW in New York. He knew who was hip. That's how I first heard notorious bad boy Chet Baker, whose trumpet and voice, along with the baritone sax of Gerry Mulligan, serenaded me with an unusual, West Coast sound that has stayed in my head ever since. All the other plump thirteen-year-old girls felt as I did. Chet needed me to take care of him. And he wore those white T-shirts. He sang songs like "I fall in Love too Easily" and "The Thrill is Gone." It was an exciting new kind of music, its cool contrapuntal sound a complete contrast to the wartime swing of Tommy Dorsey's big band and even the Stan Kenton Orchestra.

Through Jazzbo I discovered two women vocalists who became my heroes. The first was the Scottish-born Annie Ross, who had released a record in 1952 that was an underground hit. On the A side was "Twisted," a vocalese song to her shrink, the derogatory word at the time for a psychiatrist, and on the B side was the weird

"Farmer's Market" – all about beans. I learned to sing both pieces to show how cool I was to no one in particular. The second woman was Ross's friend Blossom Dearie, who had a distinctive girlish singing voice and was also an accomplished pianist. She bridged the gap between cabaret and jazz. She was known for her vocalese versions of jazz hits, particularly "Lullaby of Broadway." At one point the two women roomed together. They knew everybody in the jazz world, particularly in the New York scene, and led unusual lives for women in the early 1960s, with multiple affairs, marriages, and all sorts of "free" activity, including drug use.

    My other teacher ran a record store housed in fashionable Palmer Square. These were the only stores in town. There was the Princeton Music Shop – "The best in pops, our records are tops. Plenty of Hi-Fi, come and buy." My mother bought all her classical records and piano music there. The other store, the Music Center, was where I spent my allowance. I often dropped in on my way home, because, at the back of the store, past the bins of LPs, there were soundproof listening booths with turntables where customers could play whatever they wanted even if they didn't buy anything. The owner who wanted to be called Louie was Italian, cool and, like Jazzbo, knew all about East and West Coast sounds. He also loved to talk. He didn't care if we spent hours in the little listening booths that always smelled of cigarettes. But he didn't trust us. All the turntables were bolted down.

    He taught me more than just about records. He was older than me, but we spent a lot of time together talking about and playing music. He would put jazz records aside for me to listen to, and I learned one can feel close to someone if the relationship is built on mutual interests. It was a new kind of friendship for me.

    Which brings me back to WGBH and Father Norman O'Connor, known as the "jazz priest." Born in Detroit, he was an ordained Paulist priest and chaplain at Boston University, who wrote a weekly column on jazz for the *Boston Globe* and articles for *Downbeat* and

Metronome magazines. He also put together programs of jazz for broadcast, at first on WGBH-FM and then on the new medium of television. He interviewed big stars like Cannonball Adderley and George Shearing, the great English pianist. Shearing was blind and although he had an assistant, when he showed up at the station, he depended on me to get around the set. He played "Lullaby of Birdland" and "September in the Rain" during his interview, and so beautifully it brought tears to my eyes, and I wasn't alone. I found out he knew all about Al "Jazzbo" Collins.

When I told Shearing I loved jazz but didn't know how or where to get into that world, which seemed so male, he assured me more and more women were now performing and writing about jazz, bop, and classical music. Margie Hyams had been the vibraphone player in his quintet for years, and he and pianist Mariam McPartland, who was also English, played together on occasion at the Hickory House in New York. I asked him about the new sounds coming from Brazil. He predicted a bright musical future for it and said he had just recorded an album of Bossa Nova.

My conversation with Shearing was brief, but Father O'Connor chatted with him as if they were long-time buddies having a pint in a bar. Even in the artificial surroundings of a television studio, he always set his guests at ease, and I watched carefully to see how he did it. It was an important lesson for me to learn.

I tried my hand at all the different aspects of production at WGBH – that's the great thing about working in a small station – but only one of them really scared me. Jim was a cameraman, a friendly fellow who always had time to chat or to tell a new joke. Once I felt I knew him well enough, I asked him to teach me how to operate a camera. It looks simple, but like a lot of things that look that way, there's more to it than you'd think.

Jim's studio camera was a large machine with a seat that needed to be adjusted to the proper height for the operator to look through the lens. I had figured that out, but the device is not only clumsy it's heavy. The massive base was cast iron, designed to roll smoothly on a studio's steel floor. But the floor in our little three-camera studio was painted wood and it was uneven, so the camera dolly tended to stick and jiggle as it rolled over the cracks. I could hardly manoeuvre the beast at all, much less with the agility needed to follow a guest around the set. I practised whenever Jim had free time.

We were shooting an interview one afternoon and I was standing beside him, watching what he was doing. During a break, he turned to me and said, "Okay, your turn." As soon as the camera's red tally light went on, indicating my camera was live, I started to shake. I forgot everything Jim had told me. The image I saw through the lens was jumping and I couldn't stop it. I looked around the camera at the set to be sure. No, it wasn't shaking. It was me. I could imagine people sitting in their living rooms, thinking there was something wrong with their TV sets. I handed it back to Jim. It was not a job for me. I didn't want to be behind a camera; I wanted to be in front of it.

With that in mind, I came up with an idea for a fun program. I would host it, and best of all in those days, it wouldn't cost much. It was a fifteen-minute program called "Let's Read a Story" for children from age six to eleven. The set would be simple: a tree with a bench under it for me to sit on. Cut-out cardboard characters like Pooh, Piglet, Alice in Wonderland, and the Three Little Pigs would be arranged around the set, and sitting at my feet would be young children to whom I read excerpts from classic stories. They could ask questions about the authors, the illustrators, and anything to do with magic. I had been babysitting since my early teens and enjoyed entertaining children.

At WGBH in Boston in early 1962 on the set of the pilot for my children's show, "Let's Read a Story," although inexplicably barefoot. At just about the same time Julia Child, the celebrated author of Mastering The Art of French Cooking, *walked into WGBH and proposed a cooking show. The program director promptly lost interest in my pilot. (Photo courtesy of Dan Beach).*

There was little TV programming for children those days, and WGBH management liked the idea of a young woman hosting a show for children. They agreed to pay for my hairdo and even directed the props department to create whatever was needed for the set, which was quite a commitment for a public station with no money. Hal Pike, a talented young director, offered to take on the project in his free time. The art department made a crawl for the production credits, illustrated with drawings of characters from well-known kid's books. We rounded up a few children with the promise of lollypops and filmed the pilot program in mid-February 1962. The children behaved perfectly. In fact, they gazed up at me the same way the little cherubs had done when I was the Angel Gabriel. It all worked well. Everyone liked the program concept, the publicity photos, and the set and I was hopeful that the station would commit to it.

They didn't. The same week WGBH management screened my show, they decided to film three pilot programs about cooking. It seemed an odd choice for an educational station whose approach was more intellectual than practical, and the woman, doing the cooking was odd too. She was over six feet tall and had an unusual, wavering voice. I was told her name was Julia Child, the primary author of *Mastering the Art of French Cooking*, a runaway best seller. What none of us knew yet was that she was on her way to becoming a major celebrity and one of public television's most enduring stars. Her show got the green light, and my program idea was dropped.

She wasn't the only big name I saw at the station. For many years Eleanor Roosevelt hosted radio and television interviews on WGBH with producer Henry Morgenthau III, the son of the former U.S. Treasury Secretary, and I became used to seeing her in the studio. Their current television program, "Prospects of Mankind," described as a series of political conferences on crucial national and international issues, lasted for three seasons. Mrs. Roosevelt had a gentle voice, a courteous interviewing style, and I was often impressed when I caught a glimpse of her guests heading into the studio. Among them were Adlai Stevenson, Henry Kissinger and Newton Minow, the head of the federal broadcasting regulator, who once declared television a vast wasteland. However, the one person I would have liked to meet I couldn't. When John Kennedy, then president, did a ten-minute interview on the program on the status of women, it was done from the White House. Unfortunately for me, a special TV crew in Washington recorded that segment.

Mrs. Roosevelt was deaf, or close to it, but by using two hearing aids, rather cumbersome devices at the time, she could hear what her guest said but not the producer's voice. He had to rely on hand signals to communicate with her. Those of us on the production team had been warned that the batteries in Mrs. Roosevelt's hearing aids ran down regularly and if they did during the program, she might doze off. And she did during a program that May. As the volume of what she was hearing faded, her head slowly sank to rest gently on her chest. Her guests sitting around the studio table talked among themselves and the cameras focused on them. The end of the program was a bit awkward when the cameras pulled back for the credits, revealing the host sound asleep in her chair.

No one was embarrassed, certainly not Mrs. Roosevelt. On her way out of the studio, she shook hands with all of us, as usual. Her handshake was less than limp, but she had a lovely smile and no little charm.

As much as I enjoyed these brushes with famous people, I was becoming less enchanted with WGBH. Working there had given me confidence but no prospects – there was no path toward an on-camera career, or for that matter, a career of any sort. The cancellation of my children's show was not the temporary setback I'd expected. It had turned into a never-ending one, and anxiety about what I should be doing with my life, never far below the surface, had bubbled up. Once again, it was time for a change.

Chapter 3

Assault in Warsaw

It was a hot summer Saturday afternoon, and I was sitting in my Boston apartment looking deeply into the red wine filling most of the glass on the table in front of me. I didn't know how long I'd been staring at it, and it probably wasn't the first glass, but I knew I'd been saying to myself over and over: *Time for a change. Time for a change.* Then, suddenly, what that change should be came to me.

I loved France even more than I loved French wine. I still had contacts at the ORTF, the French broadcasting organization, I had friends in Paris, and I had recently heard about Fulbright teaching fellowships in France. Between the fellowship and money I could make freelancing, I would have enough to live on there, and better still the fellowship covered medical expenses. I applied the next day. And waited.

Weeks later, the Fulbright Program offered me a position as an English-language assistant in Etampes, a small town outside of Paris. Bingo. No need to think about that. I accepted the offer immediately.

I said goodbye to WGBH, packed up my belongings, and headed home to Princeton. My parents were not exactly pleased to see me on the move again, but prudently gave me an emergency fund to fly home on short notice if I had to. I packed warm clothes for the damp, cold Paris winter, and my record collection. I knew my contacts at the ORTF would help me find a record player and a place to live. I was happy to being going back to France. It was not as if I was a stranger and couldn't speak the language. I was sure it was a positive move, an adventure, and would have only a favorable outcome.

After leaving Paris the first time, I stayed in touch with my friend Jess, who had helped me get work at ORTF. He too had moved back to the U.S., to Niagara Falls, and it was through him that I met Marie Hélène About, who remains a good friend to this day and that is a long time. She was visiting Boston, and when Jess next came to town, she cooked us a real French dinner. I told her I had applied for the Fulbright fellowship, and, later, when she heard I'd been accepted, she suggested I stay at her house in central Paris while I looked for a place to live, and so I did. It turned out her home was a three-storey building with a back garden and a tennis court. She had never hinted she lived in a mansion.

My French friends helped me get settled. I soon found a pleasant apartment on rue Saint Sulpice, known as the street with shops for the well-dressed priest. An ad in the *International Herald Tribune* gave me a roommate, a young woman from South Africa with bright yellow hair and a good sense of humour. Two days a week, I worked at ORTF, doing the same job and on the same freelance basis as before. I enjoyed doing it, and the producers soon gave me more projects, about French history, and the arts. I was even asked to write and read the nightly radio news in English for some locally notorious man in Brazzaville I was told.

On the remaining three weekdays, I commuted to Etampes by train. The journey took an hour, and every morning the same group of men climbed into the same coaches, pushing other passengers aside, sat in the same seats, lit their Gauloises or Gitanes, and picked up their card game of belote from where they had left off the day before. They spoke to no one, not even each other, except to place their bids. I learned that belote is a thirty-two-card trick game, like pinocle, involving four participants, played mostly in France and Eastern Europe.

Teaching at the Lycée Geoffroy-Saint-Hilaire reminded me of my classes in Reid Hall for Smith College. The purpose of the Fulbright program was to promote U.S. culture overseas, so I got the youngsters to sing songs in French and English, and we talked about what it was like to be a child in France compared with a child in the U.S. With the teenage boys (taught separately from the girls), I discussed movie stars and films. Jean-Paul Belmondo's 1960 hit *Au Bout de Souffle* (*Breathless*) had made him a major star. American cowboy films were considered exotic and especially prized, although no one liked singing cowboys. Singing was not manly. John Wayne was the archetype of the Western hero, and of course he would never sing. Needless to say, the boys' favorite actress was Brigitte Bardot.

We had lively discussions in English about French popular music, particularly about the merits of Johnny Hallyday, whom the *Daily Beast* accurately described in their 2017 obituary of him as "the hip-swiveling, leather-clad Gallic answer to Elvis Presley." Johnny loved all things American: especially cowboys, motorcycles and performing in Las Vegas. A French critic described him as the biggest rock star you've never heard of. He brought rock-n-roll to France. "C'est le mashed potatoes" his song about a popular dance move, was one of his big hits. On the classroom record player, we listened to Elvis Presley's "Heartbreak Hotel" and "Love Me Tender" as well as some of my American favorites, including Mel Tormé and Billie Holiday.

At the end of the academic year, the school principal recommended a renewal of my Fulbright fellowship, which would allow me to teach at a lycée in Paris, and all eight senior boys signed their names on an EP of Johnny singing the mashed potatoes song as a souvenir of my time with them. On my last day in May, the boys gave me a memorable send off at the railway station. The group looked somewhat like the Jets or the Sharks from *West Side Story*. I climbed on the train and stood in the doorway. They all waved and yelled *au revoir* until they were out of sight. I still have the record they gave me. I still have a crush on all eight of them.

With my teaching job finished for the time being, my friends at ORTF suggested another source of freelance work they thought I'd enjoy at a well-known dubbing studio named LTC. My job would be to dub films into English, joining a small group of other English speakers at a microphone while watching the film projected on a screen. I took the job and found out quickly that the real challenge for the group was to get our voices to synchronize properly with the original voices on the film. There were different ways of cuing us but the one at LTC was called "looping." The translation of what was being said ran on a continuous loop along the bottom of the screen, and the cue to start reading was when the first spoken syllable of the actor's dialogue hit a vertical bar on the extreme left-hand side of the screen. Then it was matter of matching the movement of the actor's mouth when it was visible. An hour in the studio felt like four hours of effort but the pay was good, and our group was interesting – two Americans, two Brits, and an Irish actor. When it was all done, I watched in amazement as a Russian princess in a fur hat opened her mouth and spoke in my mid-Atlantic accent. All of us in the group became enamored by the process of dubbing and thought of it as an art.

One day we were joined by a tall, handsome young man with broad shoulders but an unusually small head, who introduced himself to us in a warm baritone voice. He kept missing his cues but eventually figured it out and then nailed his lines. We all applauded, he bowed and gave us a dazzling smile. Later we asked the producer who he was. "Sean Flynn," he said. "You know the actor Errol Flynn? He's his son." Sean was also an actor and a freelance photographer. Whenever he was on set with us, he would bring a bag of hot croissants and other pastries and we would have a picnic, then try to kick the crumbs under the table because we weren't supposed to eat in the studio.

I was surprised when he told me he'd gone to Lawrenceville, one of the fancy boys prep schools outside Princeton. He had heard of

Miss Fine's School but never went to a dance there. Later, I learned that his real talent was photography, not acting. In 1970, during the Vietnam War, he went to Cambodia as a freelance photographer and was captured by communist guerillas. He was never heard from again, and his fate is unknown to this day.

One day in May I received two important letters. The Fulbright committee had renewed my contract for another year. This time I would be teaching at the Lycée Dr. Claude Bernard, in Paris and near avenue Mozart and Madame de Renty, with whom I'd stayed in my Smith College days. The second letter was from Halina Poświatowska, my neurotic Polish friend. Halina was a noted young poet in Poland, but a complicated person, and she had a critical heart condition. We'd met at Smith. She had returned to Kraków after graduation and was now inviting me to visit her there.

I accepted although it meant a long train ride through Switzerland, Austria, and Czechoslovakia into Poland with many stops and, as it turned out, shady companions. Halina was at the Kraków station to meet me. She took me back to her one-room studio and then the drama began. She insisted that I sleep in her bed, and she would stay on the floor, because I was the guest. I didn't like the arrangement, but I didn't like the alternative, either. Not long afterward, someone knocked on the door. It was a handsome young man, Halina's current boyfriend. The next day he took me to see the sites: the Wawel Castle, the town's cathedral, and a jumble of bones said to be the remains of a fire-breathing dragon. When we returned to Halina's, she declared that she was tired, thanked me for my gift of a book of photographs of Smith College, and then told me that I had to leave because I had been sleeping with her boyfriend. I was speechless. I had not slept with her boyfriend! It was just Halina being neurotic. We said a tumultuous goodbye, and I left for Warsaw.

From the train, the outskirts of Warsaw still looked like a war zone, with rubble piled up against half-destroyed buildings. As my train got closer to the station, the railway became busier and noisier, with freight trains shrieking their whistles as they rolled past pulled by steam engines puffing out black smoke. Our train finally lumbered into the platform. By the time I got to the taxi stand, there was an acrid taste in my mouth. I noticed the same menacing-looking officers standing on street corners as I'd seen in Kraków. But the hotel Halina had recommended was a small friendly place. My quick nap there lasted for four hours. The next morning, the receptionist gave me several tourist brochures about Old Town, a bustling historical area. It had been badly bombed during the Second World War but reconstructed soon after, using rescued materials and several not entirely accurate paintings of Warsaw by Bernardo Bellotto, the eighteen-century Italian artist, for reference.

The market square was busy. There were restaurants, small stores and stalls selling crafts scattered about. Artists had propped up paintings as bright and cheerful as themselves. One young man working in front of his stall asked if he could do my portrait. I agreed, thinking it was a splendid idea. We chatted to passersby. The sun began to shine on his easel, and the young man told me we need to go to his nearby studio. It smelled of turpentine. A young woman entered and greeted me in English. They smiled at each other, and she abruptly told me goodbye and left. Shortly afterward he put down his brush and came over to the cot where I was sitting. Suddenly he was on top of me, yanking up my dress. He pulled down my underpants and I panicked. I tried to think but I couldn't. This man was trying to rape me, and there was no one around to come to my rescue. So I bit his ear lobe as hard as I could. He screamed and fell off the cot, holding his ear. I jumped up, seized my pocketbook and – in retrospect, with surprising awareness – also grabbed the portrait, and ran out onto the street. I didn't see where I was going because of my tears. At last, I hailed a taxi driver who took me back to the hotel. I was still shaking, and the wet paint had stained my dress. For the first time I looked at the painting. It was ugly. One eye drooped and the other stared ahead. The colours were black and dark red, like a ghoulish Halloween mask. I cried and cried. I hated Warsaw, there was no girl friend to talk to, no police officer with whom I could lodge a complaint.

The next day was Sunday, and I needed to be quiet and do something peaceful after my violent experience the day before. One of the tourist brochures mentioned a free concert in Łazienka Park, a pastoral spot honoring Frederic Chopin, the great Polish composer whose statue stands in the middle of the grounds. That sounded perfect, so I found my way over to the park. Near the statue was a grand piano on a raised platform, surrounded on the grass below by benches and chairs. The audience drifting in looked odd. Most were elderly couples dressed in their Sunday best, but their Sunday best appeared to be from the 1920s and '30s. Some women had lacy parasols and large feathery hats. In fact, the crowd looked as if they could have just stepped out of Georges Seurat's famous 1884 pointillist painting "A Sunday Afternoon on the Island of La Grande Jatte." Perhaps the clothing had been hidden away for safekeeping since the war years.

The soloist that afternoon was Barbara Hesse-Bukowska. My mother would surely have heard of her. She was one of the best-known interpreters of Chopin, one of my mother's favorite composers, and performed all over Europe. The music was serene, and I started to feel somewhat less anxious. During the intermission, the two elderly ladies who shared a bench with me pulled out paper bags and offered me strawberries. They spoke beautiful French. After the concert, they invited me to their house for tea. I accepted with pleasure. The building was nearby and appeared undamaged by the war. Inside was dim but filled with dark, comfortable old-fashioned furniture. They pointed out paintings that appeared to date from hundreds of years earlier. Before I had a chance to ask who these elegant men were, they volunteered that many of their relatives were born in the late eighteenth century. They were, in fact, archbishops. The ladies were proud to be related to these church nobles and felt as if they were guardians, not only of the portraits but also a part of Polish history.

During my stay in the city, I also grew friendly with a group of intellectuals who belonged to an offbeat club where they exchanged ideas about politics, drank vodka and, best of all, told jokes. It was a genuine Bohemian group of the kind my mother belonged to in her youth. I love to laugh and to make people laugh, and this was probably why they let me join. I particularly liked the joke about the postage stamp with Khrushchev's face on it. It didn't stick because people spat on that side, not the sticky side. The group who'd adopted me had all kinds of questions about life in Princeton, Einstein, my experience at WGBH and Mrs. Roosevelt's television program. They loved American films, particularly the westerns, but again not the singing cowboys. They seemed to be in a bit of a time warp, just like the audience at the Chopin concert in their vintage clothing.

When it came time to leave Warsaw, as I was waiting on the platform my new friends showed up unexpectedly carrying bouquets of roses. I burst into tears, partly because of the lovely gesture, but also because of the many emotional events I'd experienced in this country. They loaded me into the car marked Budapest, and as the train pulled slowly out of the station, I realized Poland was a very confusing place. If Hungarians are cynics, as they are said to be, then Poles are great romantics.

When I began teaching in Paris, my mother, who loved the city and wrote often about wanting to visit me, suggested she might buy a small studio where I could live, and she could stay when she came. I knew very little about real estate in Paris, but a friend said he knew a banker whom he thought would be happy to help me. He arranged for the banker to meet me a few days later, on May 1, in a café near my apartment. May Day in France is a holiday, and one of the country's charming traditions is to present your sweetheart on that day with a bunch of lilies of the valley or *muguet*.

We were to meet at one o'clock. I arrived a couple of minutes early. There were only a few people there since it was a holiday, and many Parisians had left town. I saw him right away. He was sitting in a booth at the back corner, where he could watch people coming in the front door. I looked at him and he looked at me and life froze. Everything stopped, even, for me, the traffic outside. The bartender stopped polishing the bar top and looked at me then at the man I was looking at. The few drinkers at the bar turned to follow his eyes. He smiled. I smiled. It was as if we were alone. I walked over and sat down; he handed me a bunch of lilies of the valley. Later, I remembered actress Jane Russell in *His Kind of Woman*, a 1951 film noir, singing to my favorite actor, Robert Mitchum. The song was called "You'll Know, When it Happens, You'll Know." It happened. I knew.

My life changed that day. I wasn't a girl any longer, and I wasn't fending off the groping advances of students. I was a young woman, and I was sitting with a brilliant, accomplished adult man. Jean-Jacques wasn't young or old, he was forty-four, I was twenty-six. He had laughing eyes, and he was elegant, intelligent and courteous. He reminded me of the English actor Leslie Howard.

We talked for hours about each other. After serving as a tank commander in General Leclerc's Second Armored Division, famous for liberating Paris in the Second World War, he lived in New York City for a while. He loved American movies, music, and books. He once said he loved me because I let him read. I told him about growing up in Princeton, my teaching job in Paris, studying Hungarian for the last two years at the renowned Paris Institut de Langues Orientales. After completing two years in which I took some pride in passing, I still couldn't really speak the language, but it didn't matter. My freelance work at ORTF interested him the most, and although he made his living as a lawyer and banker, he was also a playwright, and three of his plays had been performed in small theatres. He was prouder of this than any of his other accomplishments.

I met Jean-Jacques in Paris in May 1964. We travelled around France and that autumn to Ireland. We were together for six years.

He was perfect for me except in two small regards. He was married, and as I found out later, he had leukemia. At the very end of *Some Like It Hot*, Joe E. Brown looks at Jack Lemon, shrugs and says, "Nobody's perfect." It's my favorite line in a movie.

Our small farmhouse in Grand Courcelles, a village about 100km southeast of Paris, was a happy place where we spent most of our weekends.

We spent as much time together as we could, and as the months went by, we travelled a lot – in Ireland, England, and the U.S. In Las Vegas, he was delighted to see what he was convinced was a group of gangsters in colourful suits with bulging pockets. We also went to Morocco, where we watched goats climb trees to eat the leaves, to Corsica to see the troops of the Foreign Legion, and all over France. But mostly we spent time at a little farmhouse we rented in Grand Courcelles, a village 100 kilometres southeast of Paris in the district of Chevry-en-Sereine. Early every morning, about 6:30, a farmer would pass by with his horse pulling a creaking two-wheeled cart down the dirt road right next to our bedroom window. Train whistles and boat sirens were familiar morning noises for me, so the sound of a farmer talking to his horse at dawn seemed right out of a medieval tapestry.

Farms take work and our small place was no exception. Of course for really small farms, it's not worth buying machinery, so we did most of the work ourselves by hand. Or in this case, I did, shown here gamely raking tall grass.

I had to be careful about my mood swings, which I was still experiencing. I told him about my walk into the freezing Atlantic Ocean years earlier. Jean-Jacques knew of a psychiatrist who was easy to talk to. I went to see her, but her only advice about my complicated love life was to go back to the U.S. and marry a nice American. She meant well but it wasn't much help. I was always on the watch for a sign that Jean-Jacques was treating me, as the French say, "like a spare tire." He never did.

He continued to write and finally his lighthearted comedy, "Une Pincée de Soufre" – A Pinch of Sulphur – was selected for broadcast by the ORTF. It was about the legendary Dr. Faust negotiating with Mephistopheles, better known as Satan. The plot was simple. Mephisto helps Faust seduce the lovely young American, Marguerite, in exchange for the usual prize, Faust's soul. Dr. Faust and the young woman outwit Mephisto by only pretending to have an affair. Once again, Mephisto loses the battle. The woman's name was no coincidence, Jean-Jacques had me in mind to play Marguerite.

Recording the play for radio in the ORTF's dedicated drama studio was a daunting experience. The large studio was not at all like the little radio booth I was familiar with. I was surrounded by well-known French actors, the kind that have spent their lives playing characters in Molière's plays, standing in front of microphones wearing headphones. The producer, assistants, technicians, and Jean-Jacques were behind the glass in the darkened control room. There were blinking cue lights, hand signals, cryptic instructions from disembodied voices and then just as the dialogue began, the producer said, "Stop. Try that again and emphasize the first two words." And back we went.

I had never done any real radio drama work in French. Sometimes I didn't understand the directions. The French actors were relaxed. They were courteous and made funny remarks that make us all laugh. I didn't sound like a Parisienne. But my moderate Yankee accent was acceptable because Marguerite is an American character. It was challenging for sure, but at the end of the recording session everyone clapped. I can't remember if they brought out the champagne. They should have. Jean-Jacques was very happy with the final recording. So was I – and relieved.

ORTF broadcast the comedy a few weeks later. And the next day, January 7, 1966, both *Le Monde* and *Le Figaro* newspapers published reviews praising the play, the author, and the cast. I was proud to have performed in a one-hour radio play all in French, in France, to a French audience even though the papers described me as an "unknown," which of course I was. I was all too aware of my accent, and it crossed my mind that my teachers at the Smith College Junior Year Abroad program would have given me a B+, except for the phonetics professor, who probably would have made it a B minus.

It was a magical period in my life. But one important aspect I just didn't understand. Jean-Jacques spent little time with his wife and family, and rarely talked about them. Yet, despite all the time we spent together and how much we loved each other, he never once talked about leaving them.

I felt my giant mood swings returning, and I started to sink into worry and depression. Years earlier, at a gloomy moment, I had read *Back Street*, Fannie Hurst's gruesome 1931 novel about a well-educated woman who became a prisoner of love to a married man. I couldn't get it out of my mind. It wasn't the only thing.

We spent a wonderful weekend skiing in Chamonix in January 1966. Wonderful except I cartwheeled part way down the mountainside and had to enjoy the comfort, such as it was, lying on the ski patrol sled all the way from there to the local medical clinic. I had dislocated my shoulder and my knee. My skis crossed over each other and I fell forward, twisting my body. It could have been worse, as many of those who down the hillside were quick to point out. Morphine became my new best friend for a while, easing the pain.

Back in Paris a few days later, having my own *après ski* in physiotherapy, I met another physio patient, kidney specialist Doctor Charles Sachs, the only person to tell me the hard truth about leukemia. It doesn't get better, he said. Patients live only five or six years after a first diagnosis. He was very blunt and said he was sorry to tell me, but Jean-Jacques wouldn't be around much longer. I told him of our wonderful time together, but that recently he had become noticeably sicker. "If you want my advice," he said, "there's nothing you can do. Go home."

Falling down a French mountain was bad enough, but it wasn't all. Soon after our return to Paris, I missed my period. Jean-Jacques and I had a tearful discussion. Having a baby was not a realistic option. I would have loved to have his child, but such a decision presented problems, especially considering his illness. How would I care for it? I couldn't both work and look after an infant. Would I go home to Princeton as a single mother? My parents would be mortified. My mother's concert and teaching career meant she couldn't be a full-time babysitter. That was out of the question. Jean-Jacques would have to pay support. But I dreaded being financially dependent on him. The situation felt more and more like from the premise of *Back Street.* I was afraid and angry. Our relationship was fraying at the edges.

The solution was to have an abortion, and the place to go to terminate a pregnancy in those days when abortion was still illegal in France was Geneva. My Smith classmates already knew that back in 1958. It was an easy answer, but exactly where did one go and to see whom? In the end, Jean-Jacques arranged for me to see his wife's sister, who was an eminent gynecologist in Paris. That I agreed was a sign of my confusion and desperation. She received me with a cool professional manner. It was an embarrassingly awkward meeting. The examination showed I was not pregnant. I got off the examining table feeling as if a huge concrete block had been lifted off my shoulders. Yes, Jean-Jacques had proved he could take care of everything, but the scare had opened fundamental questions about our future.

I began to lose control. My mood worsened. Jean-Jacques tried to help me but couldn't. Or maybe I just wouldn't let him. All I could see was problems piling up. A narrow escape from having this baby made me realize that I loved children and wanted to have my own, but I didn't want to be beholden to Jean-Jacques, to a man whose health was visibly failing. My steady employment had disappeared during the months we had travelled around and lived in Grand Courcelles. So, I did what I had often done in the past: I went home to Princeton. I returned to New York in early June 1966 on the beautiful SS *France*. Just as we sailed out of the harbour in Le Havre, a steward brought me a telegram. Addressed to Margaret Pacsu, cabin 203, promenade deck, it read: "Tu ne t'éloignes pas, tu me retrouves." You're not leaving me. You're finding me again.

For the next two months I looked for a job during one of the hottest summers ever in a violent, dirty New York. Many of the executives who interviewed me were noticeably predatory. They lived alone in New York during the week, their families stayed in suburbs like Greenwich, Connecticut or Westchester. They called me "girlie." Too many asked me to go for a drink after work or to join them for dinner that night. I was looking for a job, but they seemed to think because I had lived in France and spoke French, I was a woman of easy virtue.

The job search wasn't fruitful. I stayed in touch with Jean-Jacques and began thinking about going back to France. He said he might be able to get a job in Washington after I told him I'd found an interesting staff opening on the French language desk of Voice of America there.

I took the exam, which wasn't difficult, and passed. They had me read news stories about race riots in the United States and conflict in the remote outposts of la Francophonie. I even read a paragraph by Victor Hugo, although I don't know why he was included. Max Bauer, a German who was head of the French operation, invited me to Washington for an interview. I thought that meant I pretty much had the job or at least was a top candidate. I was wrong. Over a cordial lunch he explained the VOA was required to meet all U.S.

citizens who pass the on-air test. Then he candidly told me about the reality of the VOA's hiring practices. The organization did not have full-time employees, it only hired freelance, temporary workers to avoid paying benefits to its staff. The French-language freelance employees who were there, were lifers. They would never resign, he said. So even when a staff position was posted – like the one I had applied for – they only hired temporary personnel. He thanked me for my interest, congratulated me, said *auf wiedersehen* and wished me well. When I told them, my parents were disappointed but relished finding out that a German was heading up the French desk at the Voice of America.

Chapter 4

Tear gassed in Paris

New York was hot and very humid. I was sitting on a bench in Bryant Park by the New York library, and after noticing it was in French, I picked up a newspaper next to me that someone had left behind. It was scarcely a newspaper – just four pages in French titled *France-Amerique*. As I scanned its pages to see what Americans were being told about France, I saw a want ad that might as well have had my name on it. "Burke Marketing Research," it read, "a small company based in Cincinnati, Ohio, wants to open an office in Paris." Okay. "The successful candidate will be trained in the company's marketing techniques and philosophy." Training? That was a word I had never heard before. I knew Paris, but I knew nothing about market research. In the public library across the street, a friendly librarian helped on that score. I applied that afternoon with a letter that included pretty much all my newfound knowledge about market research and a nod to the famous political poll devised by George Gallup, who lived not too far from my parents in Princeton.

A week later, I got a letter from Burke. I thought it was to thank me for applying. Not at all. Amazingly, to me certainly, they offered me the job – in Paris, and with decent money to boot. I accepted with indecent haste. But as it turned out I had several weeks before I was supposed to start, and I told Jean-Jacques the wonderful news. He planned a marvellous trip for us from coast to coast across the U.S.

Once more we were happily on the road. And then, once more, we had to say goodbye. He went back to Paris, leaving the words Vera Lynn sang in her wartime hit – "We'll meet again some sunny day" – echoing in my head.

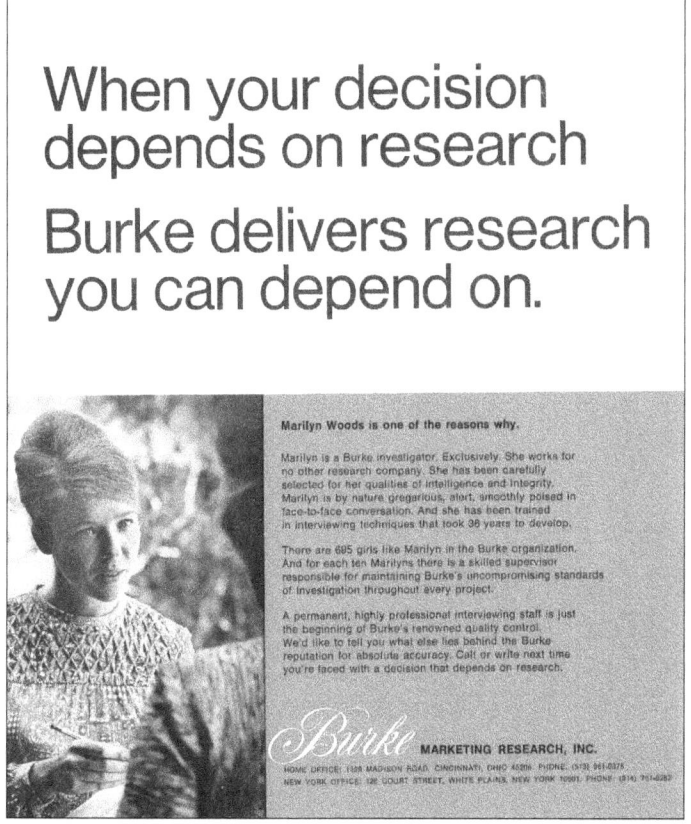

When my employer asked if they could use my image in a company advertisement scheduled for the cover of the August 1967 issue of the Journal of Marketing Research *I was flattered, that is until I saw that I had become "Marilyn Woods."*

Burke's market research program was thorough. Their slogan was "When your decision depends on research, Burke delivers research you can depend on." That sounded good to me. I started training on November 1, 1966. The company had small offices all over the country but mostly in the Midwest, and I was sent to the head office in Cincinnati, where I learned to do telephone interviews, product-placement studies (mostly giving out boxes of detergents), and lead group discussions. I liked moderating the groups, and the training gave me valuable interviewing techniques, which came in handy later.

Cincinnati wasn't Paris, but it had good restaurants – and good music. I saw the great jazz pianist Bill Evans in a smoky little bar in Newport, Kentucky, just over the border from Cincinnati. It felt almost like being back in New York. Best of all, there was a small radio station – WEBN (102-7FM) – that played classical music during the day and jazz at night. I listened to it every evening. The owner and head DJ, Frank Wood, Sr., who cheerfully referred to himself as an old beatnik, played his favorite records and talked about why he liked them. A lot of them were my favorites too. I've never been a groupie, but he sounded so folksy and engaging and knowledgeable I wanted to meet him.

I called him, and he was just as warm on the phone as he was on air. I said I'd love to meet him and, well, maybe I could help at the station. We agreed to meet a few days later. I took a taxi to the address he gave me, which turned out to be a farmhouse on the outskirts of town. It was a nice enough looking place, but just as I was telling the taxi driver not to leave, a man who, judging by the length of his hair, was the old beatnik, popped out of the barn, and waved me over. His studio was in fact in the barn. Whatever I was expecting wasn't this. He'd set up his turntables and microphone in one of the stalls. Hay still littered the uneven wooden floor. A cow gently mooed in the next stall. He pulled up a chair and there in the dim light we talked. The record covers would provide the introductions and extros to the discs. Any additional ad lib comments would be welcome. The music came first, my brief dialogue a distant second.

Later, the station moved to an old bright blue house in Cincinnati's west-side Price Hill neighborhood at 1050 Considine Avenue. People could visit the station and walk right into the studio. DJs performed live. But I was there in its very early days when the studio was in the barn. There were no people wandering around, and no late-night jazz musicians playing in combos.

Frank said he had once been a drummer in a band but couldn't tour because he had to look after his farm. I told him about Jazzbo on WNEW, the music stores in Princeton, and ORTF. After these introductions, we talked about how I could help him out. He didn't care I'd need to take occasional trips out of town for Burke or even that I'd never been a DJ or operated a live studio. Then he said, "How about Saturdays eleven p.m. to twelve-thirty, when we sign off?" He didn't have to ask twice. That was it. The next week I was on the air, and every Saturday night I was in town. The turntable was simple to operate. I sat in the semi-darkness, drank coffee, and played tracks from the albums he left out for me: big band classics, Tommy and Jimmy Dorsey, Claude Thornhill, Johnny Mercer, and some noisy, worn-out LPs of my two favorite female vocalists, Annie Ross and Blossom Dearie. I don't know how many listeners I had, or if I had any at all. But I looked forward to those Saturday nights more than I could tell and called on this experience many times in the future. It seemed like a portent of things to come.

Burke made good on their promise. Once I was fully trained, they sent me to Paris. I found a small office to rent, hired and trained the young staff, and organised the field research projects for the companies already contracted to Burke U.S.A., such as Proctor and Gamble, Ford, and French branches of American advertising agencies. Then everything came to a standstill. The anti-government protests of May 1968 disrupted life in the capitals of several countries, but nowhere more so than in Paris. There was no subway service and few buses. In the past, Parisian drivers rarely offered pedestrians a ride, but now a few would stop and offer to take you anywhere you wanted to go. I met more Parisians in that one month than in all the years I'd lived there. The heart of the turmoil was the Place Saint-Michel on the left bank, close to the Seine. I made my way down there one day to see what was going on. It looked like a scene from medieval times. The police were armed with batons and held large round shields. The youthful crowd was ripping up cobblestones, pulling the wooden boards off benches and breaking parts off parked cars, all to throw at the police. I didn't know which direction to turn. A cloud of tear gas billowed in my direction and hit hard. My eyes burned so badly I thought I was going blind. Someone pulled me into a doorway. The stinging will go away in a while, he told me. Eventually I managed to scuttle along a side street and make my way home. I was not a student anymore, and that was enough of being on the barricades to last me a lifetime.

Burke management in Cincinnati was so concerned about the rioting they insisted I close the Paris office, leaving my young employees with no choice but to go home. I was told to work out of their newly opened office in Frankfurt. I caught a bus that took me as far as the Franco–German border, where we passengers got out carrying our meagre baggage. We walked across the border into Germany, which felt very strange, and I was immensely relieved to find my Burke colleagues there to meet me. This lawlessness could never happen in Germany, they declared. I said nothing. They received me with much kindness, and I stayed two weeks, then returned to Paris to weather it out.

Management from Burke head office in Cincinnati called one day after the protests had died down to say they were coming to visit. I took this to be not a good sign. All our clients had told us they were pleased with our work, but we were still mildly apprehensive about what the visit means.

All this time, I have been seeing Jean-Jacques as much as possible. His health seemed to have stabilized, and the worries I had about becoming dependent on him were firmly in the past. Surprisingly, considering how much time had passed, he said he and his wife had discussed separating, which meant we could plan a full-time life together at last. But nothing is ever that simple. On a trip to Nice, Jean-

Jacques developed a high fever. His doctor in Paris told him to return home to Paris immediately. He was to remain quiet and in bed. Every day, I walked over to his apartment at 45 Boulevard Raspail and looked way up at his balcony. He would be standing there in his robe and wave. I, many storeys below in the open-air café of the Hôtel Lutetia, would wave back. It was heartbreaking.

Not long after Jean-Jacques developed his fever, Burke head office wrote to say they were pleased with what they'd seen on their visit and would be expanding the Paris office. Oh, and they would be hiring someone else to run it, someone with different managerial experience. Did I want to stay with the company in Paris or go back to head office in Cincinnati? My heart sank. After running the place, now they wanted me to lead field interviewers in rural France, distributing boxes of Ariel detergent? I was confused. I had worked well with all the advertising agencies that were our clients in France, and head office had regularly expressed its satisfaction with my efforts. During the May uprising they had backed me up and provided advice and support. So, what did this all really mean? Management wasn't satisfied with my performance? Then why didn't they tell me so I could correct the problems? I said nothing, but it hurt me to think they could just sideline me without any real attention to my future. Meanwhile, Jean-Jacques had received a good job offer from a bank in Montreal, so one option would be going with him and starting a new life together there. I knew it was unrealistic, just a dream, but it was hard to let go. Eventually, I decided to leave Paris and go home. Burke had a job waiting for me there, and I would have to see what it was.

Jean-Jacques took me to the airport on December 1, 1969. We hardly spoke, we were both so unhappy. On December 11, he phoned me in Princeton, and for the first time in all our years of transatlantic calls the line broke off. There were no goodbyes. A few days later, on December 15, I received a letter from him, his last.

On Christmas Day I received a telegram from one of our Parisian friends saying, "Jean-Jacques died this morning at 8:00 a.m. More information to follow. Désolés de te l'apprendre ces nouvelles." For a long time I just looked out of my bedroom window at the snow gently falling on the Magic Woods. Everything had stopped. I didn't know what to think or do. I was overcome with numbness. All I did was cry. Jean-Jacques, my best friend, my dearest love. He was forty-nine, I was thirty-two. During our six years together, we were as close as two people can be. I remembered him looking at me with a gaze of such infinite love that I couldn't move. I knew he had leukemia, but I hadn't realized how ill he was. In his last months, he said he wanted to buy the little house in Grand Courcelles where we spent so much time and give it to me. In the end, I had declined. For all our happiness, my life never did seem quite settled enough, and the cottage would never be the same without him.

Chapter 5

Abed with John Cleese

After Jean-Jacques's death, I took some time off to think about the future. Despite my disappointment at losing the job in Paris, I decided to stay with Burke. I didn't have the strength to search for a new job. Head office proved to be surprisingly understanding. They agreed running focus groups in Kansas City would not be a good fit, but would I be interested in opening another new foreign office? "Sure," I said. "Where?" In Toronto, Canada, they said. It's a quiet city, a peaceful country. I knew little about Canada except that it was neither French nor American, but a kind of in-between place. Burke had sent three of us from Cincinnati to Expo 67. We loved it and even saw Pierre Trudeau, elegant but diminutive, not yet prime minister of Canada. I found Quebec French a challenge but interesting. It seemed the right kind of place to try to recover from losing my beloved *vieux renard*. My parents knew little about our Northern Neighbor but were visibly relieved that I would be finally living on the same continent as they were.

I needed to buy a car to get there. The one of my dreams was the 1956 Oldsmobile 88, which Jean-Paul Belmondo drove in his memorable film *Breathless*. Even all these years later, it was still way out of my price range, so I settled on a cheerful blue second hand 1966 Mustang. I had never owned a car before, but with one sitting in the driveway I realized I could pack it full of my record collection, my books, and my French clothes. I stayed at Burke Cincinnati until spring.

My luck had already begun to change for the better, but I didn't begin to appreciate it until I stopped at the Canadian Customs booth at the far end of the Ambassador Bridge between Detroit and Windsor. My ordeals when crossing borders in Europe had made me apprehensive about all borders. I drove slowly to a stop and put on my warmest smile.

"Are you coming to Canada for a visit?" asked the customs officer, looking down at me from his little booth.

"No," I said, "I have a job waiting in Toronto." That was the truth, but I had no idea if it was the right answer.

He took down some papers from a hook on the wall and thumbed through the pages. Finally, he looked back at me, "Do you speak French?"

"Yes, I do."

"Do you have TB?"

"No."

He turned away, stamped a small card, and handed it to me. "You're all set, miss. Welcome to Canada." And that was that. The card was dated April 30, 1970. I thanked him, put it in my handbag and drove off to Toronto. The final and official card arrived in the mail from Windsor on July 30. Two months to the day later, I was officially a landed immigrant.

My luck continued. I bought a copy of *The Globe and Mail* newspaper, scanned the ads, and almost immediately found a small apartment in a large house in Rosedale. It reminded me of the old rooming houses in Princeton. The small Burke office was located at the northern edge of town, so my Mustang, its radio, and I spent extended time together twice a day. I had two jobs there – one as a focus group leader (which I enjoyed), the other hiring and training field interviewers – the same work I did in France. This would involve considerable travelling, an adventure in this immense country.

The first town I visited in July was St. John's, the best time of year for decent weather. I discovered Newfoundland is a very large and beautiful island off Canada's Atlantic coast. Its wild, rocky landscape reminded me of Ireland, which I had visited with Jean-Jacques. Gulls and other seabirds soared and darted above the harbour, which was surrounded on three sides by rows of brightly painted houses ranging up the steep hills. The women I had hired were eager to work as there were few jobs and they needed the money.

Newfoundlanders are a strong-willed lot, with their own ideas about how things should be done. On my first day in the St. John's office, we soon arrived at that tipping point where things could have easily turned bad, in part because I was having trouble understanding their accent. Somebody with good sense suggested we go out to eat. After a few glasses of screech, the rough local rum, cod tongues and slices of seal flipper pie, we found we understood each other quite well and enough to laugh a lot. In time, the small Burke office there became one of the most successful and loyal operations in the whole country. I think of it as my most memorable welcome to Canada.

My next assignment was the small Burke office in Quebec City. The town plunged me into eighteenth-century France. I had no idea that here in North America there was a historic town with horse-drawn carriages, gas lights, and people who spoke only French. I stayed at the imposing hotel Château Frontenac, built in 1893 on a cliff overlooking the St. Lawrence River. The town was enchanting, but no one told me that it could snow there in October. The five field interviewers I hired made it home from the hotel just before a blizzard warning was posted and heavy snow began to fall. The power went out all over the town. The hotel fell into darkness and silence. Then an emergency generator started up, providing electricity for lights, heat, and the kitchen. I joined a few of the hotel's other guests to play ping pong in what looked like the ill-lit dungeon of an ancient castle. Late the following afternoon, the snow stopped, ploughs carved narrow passages through the streets and airplanes began to take off again. When I flew out the next day, a magnificent silver-white fox ran beside the plane down the runway.

Focus groups are intended to help companies market their products – to let them know whether red boxes are more attractive than yellow boxes – but occasionally they offer some useful insight. The men in a focus group in Chicoutimi, Quebec, when the subject was companies offering payday loans, quickly decided there wasn't much to say about what approach worked best. There's no point in advertising, they said. Payday loaners are like prostitutes; you know where to find one when you want one. The client took these comments to heart.

In Winnipeg, I saw men and women huddled in doorways, drinking out of paper bags. The sessions that day were with women about street-furniture advertising, and I asked them who these people were and why they were on the street. Their reactions shocked me. Almost all of them gave out a stream of malicious words about worthlessness of the local Indigenous population. I thought for a moment I was in Alabama or Georgia. I have never heard that kind of blatant angry racism again anywhere in Canada.

A major study for General Foods just about did me in. My presentation to the corporate heads was well-received but producing the fifty-page report had been a major strain. By now I was also getting bored listening to homemakers in pastel pant suits arguing how best to get laundry clean. Writing up the focus group reports took all my energy and imagination. It was time to move on, so I started to look for another job.

One day I read that CTV, one of the only two national TV networks at the time, was auditioning people to host a new national current affairs program to be called "Canada AM." I signed up for an interview and was directed to a suburban studio not far from the Burke office. I waited for a few minutes in a small room and soon a young woman walked me into a vast, dimly lit studio. In the middle of the room was a single chair on a platform surrounded by lights and booms and

TV cameras. She pointed to the chair, so I sat on it and waited. Just as I was doubting the wisdom of all this, a voice blared out of the dark asking rapid-fire questions about my television experience, which became immediately apparent to both of us was, well, slim.

On the good side I did recall from WGBH that the red light on the top of the camera, the tally light, indicated the live camera, the one you look at. On the not-so-good side, I had forgotten it was a television interview, so makeup, hair, and elegant clothes were important. I was dressed for business, not to host a network television program. It was a short interview. The voice thanked me, and the nice young woman showed me out the front door. My Burke colleagues urged me to keep looking. So, I did.

TVO, Television Ontario, a public TV station that produced educational programs for broadcast only in Ontario, was looking for actors for children's programs. I was ready this time. My hair freshly done, stage make-up on, and well-dressed, I walked to the middle of the studio, watched for the tally lights, and played to the cameras. I read what they asked, answered a few questions, and it seemed to work. The producer said he liked it. I looked comfortable, he said. And although my pronunciation was unusual, he thought it was quite charming. I was still puzzling about what he found unusual about it as he started to describe the role he had in mind. The program would be live every day, he said. Children would be brought in. And I would be a central character – a talking bear. A talking bear dressed in a fuzzy suit. As he went on to describe the bear's character in more detail, he may have noticed my flagging interest. Or maybe bears don't have much depth of character, in any case, he went on to suggest that if I wasn't interested in the bear, I could play the friendly schoolteacher who talked to the bear.

I thanked him. He wished me well and, having read on my resume that I'd worked in France, suggested I talk to his colleagues at TVO's French-language sister station, TFO, Télévision Française de l'Ontario. I called TFO and they were indeed interested in hearing about my work at ORTF, and my experience in dubbing and translations. "But unfortunately, mademoiselle, we have no openings. And, alas, to be honest, I don't really see anything coming up."

In the meantime, two events cheered me up considerably. One day in the newspaper I came upon an announcement for try outs for the Toronto Consort Choir. Why not, I thought. I didn't know anybody, so it would be a way to meet people who share the same interests. I had spent years in the choir at Miss Fine's School (my mother accompanied us, which meant I always had to behave) as well as in an a-cappella madrigal group. At the audition, I learned the choir was conducted by David Fallis, a young man who loved Baroque and Renaissance music. He was one of the major conductors of early music in Canada and abroad, and he played ancient instruments like the sackbut and cornet. He led the Toronto Consort for years. David had me sing a piece and read a bit of music and then welcomed me into his ensemble. The choir was not composed of professional singers, like some of his future ensembles, but we performed in churches, we all loved Monteverdi and Palestrina, and our voices blended well. Our sight-reading skills weren't always up to par, but David helped us through the difficult parts. He put me in the mezzo-soprano section rather than with the high-flying sopranos. An excellent decision. I had been missing the pleasure of singing early music in a group setting. The last time had been many years earlier when I sang in the freshman choir at Smith College. But of course, there were no bass or baritone voices there. Here we had the support of those warm lower registers. I'm sure David was not aware of the positive boost he gave to a lonely young woman from New Jersey. Joining the choir was my first attempt to put down roots, as fragile they were.

For two years now, I had rented the same small apartment in Rosedale. My landlords, Martin, who had become my accountant, and his wife, Val, followed my job search, and one day mentioned a friend had a small house to sell and wanted to do a rapid private sale. Was I interested? An hour later, the owner welcomed me into his modest two-storey, two-bedroom row house. He told me the property was ten feet wide by seventy-two feet long, including a small garden. There was a porch in front and a little verandah in the rear. I naively asked whether the house had any problems. "No," he said, "unless you count an older furnace and the railway tracks, which are about a block that away." On the plus side, the subway station was just at the end of the block and there was on-street parking. I vaguely heard what he told me, but I didn't care. It was perfect. Besides, I like trains.

The neighbourhood is called Summerhill, and these row houses were built for the railway workers around 1910. The price was $26,000 – a great deal of money. The owner, an actor, wanted to sell it quickly as he had been offered a steady job out of town. He paid a modest monthly mortgage I could take over, and Martin could figure out the transfer details. We shook hands and within a matter of a few hours I owned a house. My mother gave me some money for a down payment, and my Burke salary was enough to cover the mortgage. Moving day was March 1, 1972. I loved this place. It was my own little home, and I felt much the same as I had as a child in the little room I carved out under the pine tree in the Magic Wood. I resolved to stay here and in Canada forever. No more nomadic life. No thoughts of going back to the U.S.

I didn't know much about home repairs, but I found a carpenter to build a back deck who said he could deal with a small plumbing problem too. The oil furnace looked like an octopus with multiple round ducts like the branches of a tree, but it worked. After a while I got used to the rattle of the freight trains. Only an occasional 4:00 a.m. whistle woke me up. There was only one mishap. I needed a new mattress and bought one from a wholesale dealer for a reasonable price. It was no problem to bring it up the narrow stairs and it was comfortable, offering support in just the right places. But after a while, I got itchy spots on my arms and legs, and I noticed little black streaks on the sheets, like the marks of a felt pen. There were also some on the wall behind the pillows. My Burke co-workers told me they were bedbugs, and to call Acme Pest Control. A young man arrived wearing his Acme uniform, examined my bites, the marks on the bed and told me he needed to spray the whole house. I would have to stay away for twelve hours, so the place could be closed tight. I did what he said. On my cautious return, there was an unfamiliar odour from the pesticide, but I never again had streaks on the bed or bites on my body.

    I was becoming resigned to my life of focus groups and consumer products when I heard that CBLT, CBC's local Toronto station, was looking for a story editor. It was a one-year contract job, paying less than my salary at Burke, but I decided to take a chance and ask for an interview. The CBLT newsroom was on the second floor of 500 Church Street above a Mac's Milk store, the nickname for the station. It looked just like the one in Billy Wilder's movie *The Front Page*: dark, crowded, and noisy. Reporters sat at wooden desks piled high with paper, empty coffee cups and half-eaten food, clanking away on their typewriters. A fellow came into the room with a handful of reels and lengths of video tape draped around his neck. A bank of teletype machines against the back wall clattered non-stop, the coffee machine appeared to have spilled more than it had brewed, and telephones everywhere rang constantly. Crushed cigarette butts and crumpled paper littered the wooden floor, as the few trash cans I spotted offered only an uncertain target. Cigarette smoke curled up from desks to a low-hanging blue cloud. It was unlike any office I'd ever been in. It was heaven.

    I sat on a small grey metal chair outside the executive producer's office in the corner of the newsroom and waited for my interview. I knew the drill by now. I was wearing my best French dress, the right touch of makeup, and made sure my hair looked stylish. I had a good view of the newsroom and saw what I thought were a couple of women reporters. They were the only ones. All the other reporters were men. The three other women in the room had flowers on their desks, and I took them to be secretaries. An older man wearing a suit and tie walked by. He looked familiar somehow although I couldn't say why. (It turned out he was the main news anchor). A cameraman walked in and dumped his equipment on the floor opposite me, and then another one did the same. There was a lot going on.

At last, the half-glass office door opened, and I was ushered in to meet the executive producer, Tim Kotcheff. He was a good-looking young man, businesslike but pleasant. He asked me about Burke and the interviewing I did, and about my media experiences in France. He didn't care about Smith College, but he was interested that I grew up in Princeton. He said he was looking for someone to do short TV items on economic subjects and perhaps current affairs. Was I interested? I knew little about current affairs, and nothing about economic subjects, whatever they were, so I said yes, with a smile. "That sounds very interesting."

"Great. When can you start?"

And that was it. No audition, no cameras, no awkward pauses – ten minutes that changed my life. On November 1, 1972, I started work at CBLT as a story editor. My relationship with the Canadian Broadcasting Corporation lasted twenty-four years, and I never once did a story on an economic subject.

It was not all smooth sailing, and my introduction to CBLT was shaky. Machines were the problem. They say television is like using a ten-ton lead pencil. The ten tons, of course, refer to all the machinery, most of which I never learned to use. There were chunky grey editing and recording machines everywhere, but I never got the hang of using them. Peter, the patient film editor, helped me edit all my stories for the many months I was there.

My assignments were short, human-interest stories for the second half of "News Hour," the station's daily supper-hour program. The first half was the hard news, reported mostly by men who had priority rights to cameras, editing time, travel, and the time and attention of management. They also smoked a lot and drank and swore and argued with each other, editors, managers, and anyone else who happened by. That included those of us working in the "sand box," their disparaging term for the part of the newsroom where what they called "puff pieces" were produced, mostly by women, for the second half of the program. That kind of sexism was just par for the course in those days.

Four of us produced the "puff pieces"— me, enthusiastic but inexperienced, and three senior story producers who spent a good deal of time pitching ideas for lengthy features to the executive producer and competing for airtime. My pieces usually got aired, not because of any great skill on my part, but because the senior producers' more complex stories frequently weren't ready on time. Their stories were often controversial, needed lawyering and editing; mine didn't.

My first story wasn't my strongest effort, but I learned a lot doing it. I told Tim Kotcheff about a visit to Indianapolis and how there was nothing in the city but visual clutter: used car lots, car dealerships, billboards, gas stations, flashing neon signs and fast-food chains. I said the Golden Mile in Scarborough was an example of what I meant and, if unchecked, could spread through the city. He said, "Get to it," and I did. Three of us set out in a CBC van the next morning. My crew of two – the audio technician and the cameraman – filmed more footage than we needed of the excesses of the Golden Mile, and in four hours managed to fit in two coffee breaks. Obligatory they said, union requirement. I took this to mean they needed tender care, because it's the technicians who make the reporter look great or like a goat.

Back in the newsroom, Peter edited the visual material to fit my first script, I did the voice-over, and the story closed with an on-camera shot of me saying my name and signing off for CBC News. I didn't know whether the story was any good or even whether it would be broadcast that night or bumped for something more topical. I watched "News Hour" that evening, holding my breath. The story came on. They'd said they wanted visuals, they certainly had visuals. It was under three minutes, but it was a good story, and I looked almost professional. Regrettably, the young cameraman who had done such great work filming it quit the next day to work for competing CFTO.

During my time at CBLT I produced some eighty stories. Everyone helped me find ideas. Several were memorable, not because of my presentation but because of the subject. One story seemed worthwhile but disconcerting. The Mouth and Foot Painting Artists, an organization founded in Germany in 1956, opened its doors in Canada in 1961. I had never heard of them. My crew and I set up a morning interview, but we weren't really prepared for what we found. We were eagerly greeted at the MFPA headquarters by a group of about twenty young people dressed in bright outfits who had no use of their arms. They could have been quadriplegic or had the results of thalidomide.

Painting was their primary occupation. They showed us how they sat in front of their easels holding a long brush in their mouth or between their toes. Pots of paint were lined up within easy reach. They looked contorted. The group soon realized that we felt ill at ease and tried to make us comfortable by asking us questions. They wanted our cameraman to explain how he filmed his subjects. Did he think it was art? And if so, was it as creative as their painting? He answered carefully. Yes, it could be considered as art in another medium, but it was not as personally physically creative as how they painted. The group approved his answer. I didn't dare ask these young people if they were resentful or angry about what fate had dealt them. They had already told us that their motto was self help, not charity. They were proud of selling their artwork to support the organization. As well as their original paintings, they sold greeting cards, calendars and prints of their own work and of MFPA artists in other countries. Their Christmas cards were beautiful. We left feeling far more relaxed with our new acquaintances.

When the story aired that night, the overwhelming response cheered us all, including the executive producer. After work, we all made for the Red Lion Pub on Jarvis St., our nearby friendly watering hole. The soundman and I bought our cameraman his drinks. He had earned them.

In October 1969, the BBC started to air "Monty Python's Flying Circus," a television series by a new British comedy troupe, whose skits were deliberately absurd and frequently mocked the high and mighty. All men, the six comedians – one of them an animation artist who never appeared in their skits – had attended either Oxford or Cambridge University and had formed the troupe in May 1969. Monty Python was a polarizing program. People either loved it or hated it. CBC was the first overseas broadcaster to carry the show, and aired nineteen episodes before abruptly cancelling it in January 1971 after some Christians and others took offense and wrote in to complain. Viewers who missed the program quickly made it a cause and wrote in to demand it go back on the air. The volume of mail was overwhelming, and management soon restored it to the television schedule.

In June 1973, the comedians came to Toronto to launch their "first farewell tour" of Canada because here they were idolized by huge numbers of CBC viewers. My executive producer was not among them. But after considerable badgering, and after I told him we had already booked an interview with them, he gave us a reluctant go ahead. By chance, my camera operator that day was also British. He couldn't wait for the interview. So we gathered our equipment, drove over to the Royal York Hotel, took an elevator up to John Cleese's room and knocked on the door. Cleese opened the door standing next to Michael Palin, a partner in all the madness. Both were elegantly dressed in bathrobes and greeted us warmly. The room was small and plainly furnished, certainly not the luxury one would imagine a star would insist on. There was a bureau, a table, a king-sized bed and two wooden chairs. They quickly pushed the chairs against the white wall and promptly sat on them. With nowhere else to sit, I stretched out on the bed. It was suddenly very quiet. The camera was rolling. They looked at me expectantly, heads cocked slightly, awaiting my first question. And that was what I'd been thinking about all morning. What could I possibly ask these men that wouldn't be trite or immediately mocked in a way that would make me look like a foolish young woman asking foolish questions?

I realized I probably looked vulnerable and thought since they were British gentlemen, they would not torture me. I also realized that was not much of a plan, but it was the best one I had. They waited while the silence in the small room grew oppressive. Then, in a flash of inspiration, I asked, "What question would you like me to ask?" And smiled my warmest smile. "Ah, yes," said Cleese, looking at Palin while they answered in unison, "Ask us what humor is." So, I did. They jumped into an answer as if a starter's pistol had gone off. It ended in a non-stop eight-minute simultaneous discourse in English, German, Latin, Gaelic and possibly gibberish. It was incomprehensible. But at the end, they seemed really pleased and we all laughed. They stood up; the interview was over. Come again, they suggested, as if they really meant it. Back at the station we showed the tape to executive producer Tim Kotcheff. He hated it. A plain white wall, with two peculiar Brits banging on in foreign languages and who knew what else, but it went to air anyway to the delight, I was told, of Python fans.

While working at CBLT, I only had one odd but scary confrontation, which still makes no sense to me. I had been there for a few months and knew pretty much everyone – some were friendlier than others, of course. But one time when I passed one of the senior cameramen in the hall, I smiled at him and heard him say what sounded like a vulgar word. I wasn't sure. But the next time, I was. He was calling me a vulgar name every time we passed. Then it turned more public. He took to insulting the way I looked and my American accent and ridiculing me in front of my colleagues. It was hurtful and puzzling because I had no idea why he was so angry about me. There was always jocularity in the newsroom and even some ribaldry, but this was different. There was no fun here. Still, no one in the newsroom rose to my defence and told him to leave me alone. He was a large man, with a stomach that spilled over his belt. Within a few weeks, he was regularly looking for occasions to walk past my desk, lean down, and spew his insults. Everyone has a limit and mine came the afternoon he blocked the door to the office and started on his by now familiar insults. When he got to a sexually explicit word, I hit him. Closed fist to the mouth, powered by weeks of anger and humiliation. I expect it hurt. It certainly hurt my hand. But he backed away, and I walked with trembling knees to my desk. Everyone in the newsroom saw the confrontation. There was silence. We avoided each other after then, except for the time he knocked at my front door and, without a word of explanation for his previous hostility, handed me a bouquet of flowers.

Chapter 6

Joining the CBC's RAF

I had been at CBLT in Toronto for just over a year and a half when Tim Kotcheff called me into his office with a proposal. He told me there was an announcer position opening at the English network level, a permanent staff job. It would mean a variety of opportunities in radio and television, both local and network – from coast to coast to coast, as the CBC likes to say. A staff announcer must be knowledgeable enough and capable of doing everything from live television news and celebrity interviews to reading the late-night marine weather forecasts. The CBC had twenty-nine network announcer positions at the time, no more and no less, twenty-eight of them were held by men. There was only one woman staff announcer, Jan Tennant, an elegant and very capable woman who would become a good friend.

The position had just opened because the young man who had filled it for the past few years had taken a job with one of the three major American television networks. This had raised some eyebrows because the offer he'd accepted was with a game show. Alex Trebek took the job anyway and went on to host "Jeopardy," the now legendary game show, for the next thirty-seven years. I'd heard his name a few times in the office, although I never met the man. Unbeknownst to him, I took his position and so owe my career to the good judgement of that American producer who thought, correctly, this CBC announcer would make the perfect host for his new game show.

Reading the news on radio or television, interviewing celebrities, and VIPs, hosting music programs; the more I thought about it the more I realized this was the job I had been waiting for all my life. It could be almost fun.

I already knew the names of some of the other announcers because I'd seen them on television or listened to their programs. Harry Mannis, George McLean, George Finstad, Lloyd Robertson were staff announcers at the time, and all possessed beautiful, rumbling voices and a few had the elegant RAF-style moustaches, just like BBC announcers.

Music programs? Well, I knew something about classical music, having heard it at my mother's knee, I loved jazz, and of course I'd listened to pop music on the radio for years here and in France. I didn't know much about country music and certainly not Canadian country music, and nothing at all about Maritime fiddlers, but I figured I could learn. Opera would be a problem, though. I didn't know anything about opera. And to say I wasn't a fan would be an understatement. I only hoped I wouldn't be asked about it and no one would notice.

With that consideration in mind, I thanked my executive producer, and after asking directions several times found the radio building on Jarvis Street, signed up for the staff announcer test. I returned several days later, and Ken Haslam, one of those men with a deep resonating voice and fighter-pilot moustache, walked me down the hall and held open the door to a small studio. He motioned for me to sit behind the wooden desk in a room barely big enough to hold it, handed me three typed pages titled "CBC Announce Test," and walked out. Moments later he reappeared behind the glass in the adjacent control room and pointed at the headset sitting on the desk next to me wrapped around an overflowing black ashtray the size of a dinner plate. The headset looked like the kind you see radio operators wearing in war movies as they hammer out a desperate SOS – a spring metal band connecting two black Bakelite pucks that covered your ears, and a wire plugged into a box on the desk. I put it on gingerly and he asked me to say something so he could get a level. He came back to adjust the microphone a few times and then we started the test.

There were grammar questions, words and sentences in foreign languages, largely unheard-of place names, the names of past and present politicians, composers, musicians, and a long list of words that are often mispronounced – "mischievous" and "anemone" and the like. It took about an hour, and it was stressful. In the end I understood why the ashtray was so big and so full. If I'd had any cigarettes, I would have smoked too.

I thought the test went well. It helped that I was fluent in French and knew enough of a few more languages that I could pronounce the words. And I knew most of the proper names of places, not all though, and I stumbled through "Attawapiskat" and "Tamagotchi." Fortunately for me, even the old CBC announcers who made up the test weren't mean enough to include the country's longest place name, Manitoba's Lake Pekwachnamaykoskwaskwaypinwanik. (Cree, I'm told, meaning "where the wild trout are caught by fishing with hooks.")

A few days later, I received inside an interoffice mail envelope the letter that changed my life. It didn't say much except that I had passed the test and to please indicate by return interoffice mail whether I wanted to accept the announcer position.

Of course, I wanted it, and I accepted the offer right away. Some months later, I found out that it was a closer thing than I had imagined. A committee of three men and one woman had listened to my test tape. My knowledge of music and musicians, politicians, and overall voice quality was good, they thought. My knowledge of geography and place names was acceptable. The three men said they liked what they heard, however, the woman on the committee was hesitant. She wasn't sure why she was doubtful, but finally settled on my Italian pronunciation, which she said was poor, which it was. The discussion had ended when one of the men asked her, "And how is your Italian pronunciation?" My passable German, smattering of Hungarian and fluent French got me the job even though my accent was French, not Quebecois. I was the second woman hired as a staff announcer for the network.

The red brick building in downtown Toronto on the west side of Jarvis Street was built in 1898 to house the newly founded private girls boarding school, Havergal Ladies College. It was a rambling structure on a street once lined with gated mansions and reminded me of Miss Havisham's spiderweb-filled mansion in *Great Expectations*. The CBC bought it during the Second World War, but it was used by code breakers and spies until the war was over and the CBC could move in.

Not much had changed in the years since then. The original chapel, used during the war as a gym for spies to practise their deadly arts was now a large drama studio, where the likes of John Reeves and J. Frank Willis produced dramas written by W.O. Mitchell and Lister Sinclair. The basement swimming pool, mention of which was still regularly used to entice prospective employees, had long ago been boarded over and turned into a workshop; the now dry pool a convenient place to store wood. More than one of the technicians who worked there talked quietly about seeing the ghost of a young student who had drowned in the pool. The studios were on the ground floor in what I expect were the old classrooms.

What hadn't been changed was the building's rabbit warren of small rooms on the upper floors. Once student bedrooms, they were now offices. The News and Current Affairs departments took up the lower floors, the music department, which I came to know well, was on the third floor, just below the gabled attic space, where most of the narrow offices had sloped ceilings so steep that standing upright was possible only in the middle of the room. Those who said CBC was slanted were right, but it was the music producers who walked with a list to one side, not the news people. And no matter where you were in the building, the odour from the basement cafeteria was never far away and rarely appealing. The building also smelled of cigarette smoke, old wood, and floor polish. There were large red fire axes hanging on the walls that more than once, I was told, had been plunged into a wall in a fit of anger. Hoses and fire extinguishers were everywhere – a sensible precaution for a crowded, old, wooden building full of not very careful smokers.

My office was on the main floor near the front entrance. It was a good-sized, almost windowless room furnished with threadbare stuffed chairs, a couple of dusty chesterfields and two small cigarette-burned desks. It wasn't exactly all mine. It was the announce office, the room I shared with the twenty-eight other staff announcers, twenty-seven of them men. The sole woman was Jan Tennant, who, I learned later, had been promoted to the position in December 1970. What was mine – at least I thought it was, since it was the only one without a name – was a pigeonhole in a wooden chest on a table just inside the door. That's where producers left scripts or messages, and the mail boy (for that's what he was) came by twice a day with letters, memos, and work schedules.

The door was always open, but it was widely understood that only announcers were allowed inside. If there was any question about that, Dorothy Whyte, who sat at a desk facing the door, would make it clear in a motherly sort of way that the office and the announcers were hers and she was there to protect them. After I got to know her, she told me that in the 1940s she used to sing with big bands, such as Lucio Agostino's and later as a guest vocalist with Percy Faith, who changed popular music in the 1950s by replacing the brass section with a full orchestra. She was the widow of the widely regarded sportsman, writer, and broadcaster King Whyte .We also had an announce supervisor, who used an office tucked away in the back corner that was barely big enough for a desk. He reviewed our performance, wrote "confidential" letters for our personnel files, and put handwritten notes about performance deficiencies into our pigeonholes. He was so prim, he could have been a holdover from the old Havergal Ladies College.

I took up my new position on the announce staff officially on March 24, 1974. When I walked into the office, Jan Tennant welcomed me warmly and offered to introduce me to the other announcers lounging around there. Some stood up to shake my hand. One of the small-mustached men lowered his newspaper enough to look us up and down. "Well, well," he said in his deep resonant voice. "So you girls are taking over." A few men laughed, but Jan and I just smiled. We knew, as Bob Dylan said, the times they were a changin'.

It might sound like an easy job: sit there in the quiet semi darkness of a studio and read the large type of a script someone else has written. No distractions, no memorizing, no preparation, a few minutes work, and you're done. I knew it wouldn't be exactly like that, but I hadn't expected it to be as harrowing as it was. The first time I was scheduled to read the late-night network news, on March 26, just two days after I'd started, I was given a studio number, and around 10:50 p.m. I walked down the quiet hallway and pushed open the heavy studio door. I was alone. I sat at the small table and watched the second hand sweeping around the big clock face in front of me. Six minutes before I was to read my first network radio news, I was still the only one there. I went out into the hall and checked the studio number.

I didn't know what to do or even who to call, since I'd never done it before. But a minute later, I saw the door to the control room open, and the news producer and technician walked in. I smiled, the producer didn't. He pointed at the earphones on the table, motioning for me to put them on. They looked the same as the ones I'd worn for my audition a week ago and were just as sticky. When they were uncomfortably on, he said, "Give me a level," I said "Test" a couple of times, and the technician rushed in to move the microphone, which was intricately suspended from the ceiling above me, closer to my mouth. He left as wordlessly as he had come in. I looked at the producer, shrugged politely, and asked where the script was. He wasn't looking at me, and I asked again before realizing he couldn't hear me.

In four minutes, I'd be on the air, I didn't have anything to read, and I couldn't get the attention of the people in the control room. I started to panic. What should I do? Just talk? Not say anything at all. Hundreds of thousands of people would be listening to me or to complete silence.

I'd received no training. When I'd asked, the announce office said the news producer and technician would show me everything I needed to know. Nothing to worry about. Although I had recorded many dubbings and my little pieces for ORTF in France and had at least walked through the CBLT television studio several times, this was only my second time in a radio studio. And so far, no one had given me the tour – although I'm not sure two people would have fitted in the announce booth at the same time – or had even shown me which button to push to turn the mic on and off.

There were three minutes to go to what I was expecting to be the most profound embarrassment of my life. My eyes were fixed on the second hand continuing its sweep. By then I was certain mine would be the shortest announce career in CBC history. I was on the verge of bolting for the door when it flew open again and the producer handed me the script. "Get out at seven twenty-five," he said, "and then a thirty-second weather."

I looked through the sheaf of green pages, one story to a page, all in large type, some with words crossed out, carets and arrows to inserts. Before I could read through the first couple of stories, I heard the producer say "five seconds" in my ear and then I looked up from the script just in time to see him pointing at me. The mic light flashed on, and I was on the air. Live, sweating, and panicky.

I'd like to say it was smooth sailing after that, but things did not go well at all. I stumbled through one story after another, short of breath, my hand shaking the pages loud enough for listeners to hear. I couldn't watch the clock and read at the same time, so seven minutes and twenty-five seconds came about midway through the last story. I know that because I saw the mic light go out.

I heard the producer say, "Weather at the top." The news was national, but the thirty-second weather forecast that followed was provincial, Ontario in my case. It was a nightmare. The first forecast was for Pickle Lake, and then Kapuskasing and Manitouwadge followed by Port Severn, Attawapiskat and Kashechewan. There are many First Nations in northern Ontario, and they may well have depended on the CBC for the forecast, but I doubt that any of them recognized the name of their community as I pronounced it.

After the mic light went off, I slumped in the chair, shaking. It was the longest eight minutes of my life. The producer said nothing. He made no comment on what I saw as an epic disaster and left the control room. The technician sat at the board reading a book. He didn't say anything either. I tried to comfort myself by thinking that no one was listening at that time of night. But that didn't work. Of course, they were listening.

I did somewhat better at midnight and 1:00 a.m., when I had to read the same news and weather report again. The producer and technician were no more helpful, and I was still rattled, but at least I'd had time to rehearse the stories and puzzle my way through the place names.

I went into the office the next day fully expecting to be reprimanded for my embarrassing performance. I wasn't, as it turned out. I didn't hear a word. Maybe nobody was listening after all.

That's not quite true. I did hear from one person – fellow announcer Allan McPhee, a small man who wore glasses with heavy black frames, an unlikely iconoclast who relished mocking his bosses, especially on air. Allan had joined the announce staff in 1937 and worked with the satirist Max Ferguson (aka Rawhide) for years and then for many more every evening on his own show, "Eclectic Circus." The many stories about what Allan McPhee had said and done were legendary and gleefully passed around. It was Allan who waited until the coldest winter day to pelt his hated neighbour's car with eggs, and who once ran a hose from his car's exhaust into what he thought was the office window of a fellow announcer he disliked. It was the wrong office.

I was walking down the hall the next morning with some trepidation when I heard him call my name. He asked how I was, said he had heard me the night before, said he didn't like that night shift very much and complimented me on my "imaginative" pronunciation.

It could have been much worse, of course, but as it turned out that was the only time I was asked to read the late-night network news and weather. The news producers didn't ask for me again.

Chapter 7

Bad weather for bunnies

As a member of the announce pool, I could be sent anywhere an on-air voice was needed, but I also had weekday assignments. My first regular one – although more by accident than plan – was hosting a one-hour afternoon classical music program, "Divertimento," broadcast on CBL, the AM station, which could be heard throughout Ontario.

One afternoon, I was in the announce office when a young man with a beard hurried in, looked around, and saw me sitting on the well-worn chesterfield.

"Do you know anything about classical music?" he asked.

"Yes, I do," I said.

"Then come with me."

I followed him down the hall and into one of the music studios, where Jan Tennant was sitting at the table with a small pile of LPs in front of her – and a box of Kleenex. She had a terrible cold and was so hoarse she couldn't talk. She stood up, croaked, "It's all yours," and left the studio.

The young producer apologized for the short notice and introduced himself as Fredd Radigan.

"What's your name?" he asked. I told him.

He said the record covers were in the order the music would be played. "You'll have to do an intro and extro for each cut," he said.

"Just make up whatever you can."

We went to air eight minutes later. That was enough time to read the first cover and while that piece was playing, I read the next one. So it worked out okay. I always found something to say, and the hour raced by. My improvised performance wasn't perfect, but it was a lot better than when I read the late-night radio news and weather.

Fredd professed himself happy with the result. When I told him my mother was a concert pianist and I had grown up with her practising several hours a day, he said it would be a help to have someone who could pronounce the names of Hungarian violinists, composers, and conductors correctly. A limited endorsement, to be sure, but he asked, if it was all right with Jan, whether I would like to host the program regularly. Afternoon classical music beat the nightly news any day, I thought, so I said yes. Jan also thought it was an excellent idea, especially as it would protect me from the late-night radio shift, and so Fredd and I began our one hour of classical music. No one really noticed the show, a regional broadcast, on air at four o'clock weekday afternoons, but Fredd and I got used to working with each other, and I hosted the program for a year.

Jan not only gave me this program, but she also broke the trail for me and all the women announcers who followed us. She had started at the CBC in 1966 as a secretary at CBLT, the local Toronto station, and for four summers unsuccessfully auditioned for a staff announce position until she was hired as the CBC's first female announcer. The second wave of the women's movement was in full swing in the late 1960s, and the Royal Commission on the Status of Women had published its report in 1970, so most CBC managers recognized the inevitability of bringing in more women. That didn't mean they liked the idea. Women were okay for some positions, music programs were a good place, but not the news. Women's voices were deemed to lack the weight and authority needed for reading the news – they were too high and too light.

That was neither right nor fair, of course, but at the time there wasn't much in the way the CBC treated Jan and the few women staff producers that was fair. It wasn't as dramatic as walking into a men's locker room, but we women were welcomed with little enthusiasm. We were tolerated. It wasn't uncommon to be patronized or disrespected – the kind of sexism, even misogyny, that today would result in instant dismissal. Many thought that if we found it difficult to work there because the men were upset, we should go somewhere else.

Winning recognition there first meant having to battle for it. But Jan was up for the fight and never backed down. She has an indomitable spirit, energy, and a healthy belief in her own value. She took strong positions and usually won. She warned me which managers and producers to stay away from and tipped me about the few male chauvinist announcers.

Both Jan and I had had complicated romantic relationships in our mid-twenties, and we had both spent several years in different career areas, me in marketing research and she as a high-school gym teacher, a position we joked was good preparation for her current job. We never competed at work, which is perhaps why we are still friends after so many years. We did play tennis though, and she was good, winning every game with a strong slam that just dribbled over the net onto my side.

She was the first woman to read "The National' on CBC TV. At the time, and perhaps still, it was the most prestigious news job at the CBC. She went on to read it regularly and was a hero to us all. But it started by chance.

In 1974 George McLean, a man of considerable elegance and unmistakable authority, possessed of a square-jaw and a neatly trimmed mustache, and who also had one of the best voices for news reading I've heard, presented the TV news five nights a week with an air of unmistakable authority. George Finstad, an announcer without a neat mustache but with a similarly authoritative voice, read it on the weekends. Each, when necessary, would replace the other. It was an arrangement that worked well until Easter weekend, 1974, when the two Georges asked for time off to play in a charity golf tournament. The producer agreed but was left with the problem of a replacement.

To his credit, some months earlier he had approached Jan with the suggestion that she might fill in on an occasional weekend, as a backup. Jan said she was interested, of course, but hesitated out of concern that this was tokenism, a publicity gimmick and not a serious offer. With the Easter weekend fast approaching, he asked her again if she would fill in for George. Still doubtful, but not wanting to turn it down flat, she said she would think about it and get back to him, although she never did.

So that Saturday morning, she was very surprised when she picked up *The Globe and Mail* that her partner had tossed on the bed next to her to see her picture on the front page under the headline: "First woman newsreader on CBC National news."

She told me that a wave of anxiety had washed over her, the first of many that weekend. At 9:00 p.m. Easter Saturday 1974 and the following day, Jan Tennant read the news. She was nervous, to say the least, but she got through both newscasts without a mistake, even though there was no autocue, just a sheaf of green paper, each sheet with a typed story and spaces indicating when to stop for filmed reports. As momentous as it was for her and all of us, the world didn't stop spinning when she appeared, and the audience reaction the next day was all positive.

After that, she read "The National" often and sat in for other announcers who weren't available on weekends and then during the week as well. She did other on-air work at the same time. It was stressful for her to be the centre of this new attention being paid to the CBC, and she came to feel her work was not being appropriately represented in her paycheque. She asked CBC for more to bring her pay more closely in line with the other newsreaders on "The National." CBC refused. So, after eight years reading the news, at the end of March 1982, Jan left for Global Television, where she partnered with Peter Trueman reading the Global national news. The arrangement didn't last long. After two years, Global sent Peter to Ottawa to anchor the first half hour of the program, the news, which – when the House of Commons was sitting – was largely serious political stories, interviews, and analysis. Meanwhile, Jan was to stay in Toronto and host the back half of the program, the soft stories.

After five years, in the spring of 1987, Jan retired from Global Television. She and her long-time partner, award-winning CBC documentary producer George Robertson, moved to Vancouver. Her pioneering role in broadcasting has never been properly recognized.

Judy Maddren also started at the CBC in 1972. She, Jan, and I weren't exactly the Three Female Musketeers, but early on we certainly had similar experiences, shared some personality traits, and bridled at the often-displayed ignorance of CBC management. Judy is a few years younger than Jan and I but is just as resolute.

While Jan and I sampled other careers before finding CBC, Judy said she knew that she wanted to be a CBC announcer when she was a teenager. The multitude of voices, the ideas, and range of music she heard on CBC Radio had captured her imagination. What she heard was lively, exciting, and she wanted to be part of it. So at age fifteen, she wrote a letter saying how much she loved CBC Radio and asking about job openings. To her amazement, a few days later she received a reply thanking her for her interest. "We have many talented girls at the CBC," the letter assured her, but it continued, "working as production assistants and secretaries." Until then she hadn't noticed that just about all the voices she heard on the radio were men's.

She graduated from the University of Guelph in the late 1960s with a degree in consumer studies. Her desire for a career in broadcasting undaunted, she wrote her undergraduate thesis on women at the CBC. There were a few. She asked two of them if she could talk to them about their experiences in the media and both agreed. Ruth Fremes was the author of a series of popular books about food and nutrition and from 1960 to 1972 host of a cooking show first on CBC

Radio and then on CBC Television. In 1972 she moved to CTV, where for the next ten years she hosted a half-hour cooking program named after her series of cookbooks, *What's Cooking*. The second woman was Joan Watson, a consumer advocate, who at the time hosted "Consumer Report," a weekly CBC program for homemakers. In 1972, she created "Marketplace," a program still on CBC today, and co-hosted it for some ten years with George Finstad.

Both Jan and Judy were first hired as secretaries, but by 1972 the Corporation had started to offer women short term contracts as television story editors, and Judy got a job as a researcher in consumer affairs, based in Ottawa. Doors were opening a crack for women, if slowly, and Judy did manage to get on the air. When her boss asked her if she would like to read the radio news, she immediately said yes. Of course, she would. Although as it turned out, the job was not exactly high profile. She read the news on the Northern Ontario LPRT chain, a three-minute broadcast every hour. CBC is mandated to broadcast to all Canadians but long ago realized that building radio stations in the vast sparsely populated areas of the country was not economically feasible. Instead, it built small, short-range transmitters – low-power relay transmitters – to broadcast its signal. You may have seen one: a grey metal box with an aerial next to it in an elevated location surrounded by a chain link fence. There was no glamour in being the newsreader for any of the northern relay chains, but the broadcasts were important, especially the weather forecasts, and Judy heard from fans scattered through Northern Ontario.

There was glamour of a sort in being a television weather announcer, although the men in the newsroom were known to call the women doing it "weather bunnies." It was an unnerving job, and even hearing about what was involved was enough to drain the blood from my head.

The evening television weather report was done live, with no teleprompter and no script. Just a marker and a map. Weather data came in on a teleprinter, one of maybe eight or nine that constantly clattered away at the back of the newsroom. Judy had to find where the areas of high and low pressure currently were, how the fronts were moving, the areas of precipitation, temperatures, and wind directions and the forecast for all of them for the next day. And then memorize it all. When the light on the top of the camera flashed red, she had to draw the systems on a blank screen and write the current and forecast temperatures for the major towns. Amazingly, to me anyway, she always said it was something she enjoyed.

While Judy was stationed in Ottawa, she met her future husband, Anglican minister Tim Elliott, who was based in Toronto. The CBC had a trunk line between the two cities so they could call each other without charge. In the spring of 1976 Judy decided to move to Toronto where her persistent efforts resulted in her being hired on staff that fall for the taxing newsreader's position on CBC Radio's "The World at Eight" (soon renamed "World Report"). The job meant Judy had to be in the radio studio at 6:30 in the morning. She read the first edition at 7:00 a.m., which was 8:00 a.m. in the Maritimes (and 8:30 in Newfoundland and Labrador). Altogether, she presented the news broadcast in five time zones. This was difficult enough, but by then she and Tim had married and moved to King City, a lovely community some forty kilometers north of Toronto, where he was pastor of the local Anglican church.

After their first son, Jeremy, was born Judy resigned her staff position and for the next fifteen years worked at CBC but without a contract. Whenever they needed a shift filled, they called Judy.

Like mailmen, newsreaders must get through, to the studio in this case, despite rain, wind, snowstorms, or traffic accidents. From 1980 to 1988, Judy drove to Toronto in the early hours of each weekday morning and never missed a freelance assignment. She earned the admiration of all of us. She never complained about the hours in the studio or the stressful traffic jams that could have caused her not to show up nor her irregular schedule.

Judy hosted a children's program for one season at a time when she was pregnant. Dorothy Whyte, who looked out for all three of us, insisted that Judy lie down between shifts on the old, faded sofa in the announce office. She also demanded that the men stop smoking whenever Judy was in the room. CBC management in its wisdom felt at five months she could no longer host the children's program because she was, well, with child. She decided it was time to leave the corporation to look after her growing family and, as she told me, to be the wife of a priest.

In 1993, Judy was invited to rejoin the CBC as a full-time staff announcer to host or co-host the morning news program, "World Report," and took on an additional prestigious job when she replaced Russ Germain as the CBC broadcast language advisor. It involved providing, maintaining, and updating pronunciation guidelines and offering critical feedback to all on-air staff announcers. The BBC had had a similar service for years. Mysteriously, to me at any rate, management decided Judy should be replaced by a committee which meant no one person was responsible for checking up and following through on our mistakes.

She also took on the evening radio news broadcast, "The World at Six." It started off as a solo role but soon a male announcer was placed in the opposite chair. After all her years of experience she found it demeaning. As with Jan Tennant, CBC management never felt comfortable with women in solo positions handling the news alone. She signed off for the last time on March 17, 2009. To my knowledge Judy Maddren is the only female announcer to have been offered and accepted two staff positions during her career at CBC.

Chapter 8

Why you shouldn't talk too much to Margaret Atwood

"Divertimento," the afternoon classical music program I hosted from April 1, 1974, to October 1975 was fun to do, but it took little more than an hour a day in the studio, leaving me available for other assignments. That usually meant filling in for a sick or holidaying host, reading hourly news broadcasts or maybe intros and extros on other music programs. At the time, there were some twenty-two unions representing the various groups of CBC employees, announcers were in one of them. By contract, only announcers could read news stories, host music programs and just about every program that came out of a CBC studio. Shop stewards made sure the rules were strictly enforced. It meant that, on occasion, we were given work we had no experience doing.

That's how I ended up doing my first television interviews. The regular host of a weekly television arts program was sick and since I was available, I was assigned, despite my lack of experience, to interview the show's three guests that week. The story producer dropped off an envelope for me with a page of questions, some typed notes on the people I was to meet, and a few newspaper stories pasted to sheets of green paper pulled from the CBC's reference library files. The first interview was scheduled for the next morning. That was more than enough time for me to develop a decent wave of unhealthy anxiety.

The following day, I had been in the makeup room for twenty minutes or so, reading newspaper clips and background information about my first interview, when she arrived. The producer thought the two of us would get along well. She was a rising literary personality, already popular among readers our age. When she walked in I was immediately struck by her warm smile and her wonderful curly hair. She settled into the chair next to mine, and the makeup artists quietly went to work on both of us. After a while we forgot about them.

Her name was Margaret Atwood, and she was here to talk about her career. We quickly introduced ourselves and I asked her brief questions about her literary work. She published her popular first book of poetry *The Circle Game* in 1964. Her first novel *The Edible Woman* was released to considerable acclaim in 1969 followed by *Surfacing* in 1972. We spoke briefly about her thoughts as a writer of both poetry and fiction. I brought up *Surfacing*, which I had read recently. I told her I thought it was an unsettling narrative about separation, reflected in personal relations, much like the difficult political situation unfolding between Quebec and the rest of Canada. The image of water (my astrological sign) helped me empathize with its complex characters. No comment from Margaret. We quickly changed the topic, started talking about our lives and discovered that at times we had followed parallel paths. We both had attended a prominent east coast women's school in the U.S., I at Smith College; Margaret at Radcliffe College, where she earned a master's degree in 1962.

We both loved Boston and reminisced about Cambridge and the Harvard Yard. She'd spent time teaching at Harvard before going to France in 1970 and 1971. I had recently come to Canada after six years in Paris. Margaret was the first person to understand what it means to spend that much time in La Belle France. We had begun to reveal somewhat more personal details to each other when the floor director called us to the set. The lights were already on, we took our seats, the microphones were in place, and we did a sound level check. All was good. The cue light flashed. We sat there looking at each other. She waited for me to ask a question, but nothing came to mind. We had already said it all. We smiled, and the silence stretched for hours, although it didn't, of course. I did finally come up with some questions, and she answered graciously. We both looked elegant, but the interview was short. All I could think about was the two of us going to a café where we could share a bottle of wine and continue talking about France. That never happened, but I've followed Margaret's career closely and remember with pleasure she was my first television interview. I did learn one lesson, though – never talk at length in the make-up room to the person you are about to interview before the cameras are rolling.

The next day, I had another interview scheduled. The conversation with Margaret Atwood had been friendly, but this one was downright painful. David Clayton-Thomas, a Toronto musician best known as the singer-frontman for the jazz-rock group Blood, Sweat & Tears, was in town promoting his solo album from 1973, *Harmony Junction*. It had been well received by the critics but although I'd listened to it several times it wasn't music I liked or understood. And maybe that showed more than I thought.

I was already on the set, dressed in one of my prettiest French dresses, when Mr. Clayton-Thomas walked in.

He was a burly man, tattooed, bearded, and wearing sunglasses. He glanced around the studio as if he didn't want to be there, and the look he gave me was dismissive – as if I was about as with it as his mother. The technician clipped on his mic, and he ignored the director's request for a sound level. He finished smoking his cigarette and immediately lit another. In a recent story, he'd said he was tired of touring. I asked a couple of probably dull questions about what it's like constantly living on the road, which he barely acknowledged. He was there to talk about his 1973 solo album, so I skipped over the preliminary questions and got to the question a lot of fans were most interested in. "You've been enormously successful with Blood, Sweat & Tears, are you ever going to rejoin the band or stay solo?" He stared at me for a moment and answered: "I don't know." And with that he unhooked his microphone, stood up, stamped out his cigarette on the floor and, without a word, walked off the set and out of the studio. I felt embarrassed, but relieved. This kind of encounter eats away at one's self-confidence. The TV director and the crew laughed and said to forget about it. Easy for them to say. I didn't find out for years that Clayton-Thomas had troubled relationships with the U.S. and Canadian governments, which perhaps made touring decisions as the star of a rock band like Blood, Sweat and Tears difficult.

The same afternoon as the Clayton-Thomas almost-interview, I was also scheduled to interview a man about naked women. The interview had nothing to do with music or to most minds even art. It was with photographer Bob Guccione, founder of *Penthouse* magazine, which was, well, more revealing than its competitor, *Playboy*. The story producer warned me he had a reputation for being volatile, cold, and detached. Great, I thought, another moody man. How lucky could I be? The early 1970s was the period when various magazines competed for attention and sales by publishing sexy photos of nude men and women. I had glanced at Hugh Hefner's *Playboy*, looked at Burt Reynold's iconic photo in *Cosmopolitan* in April 1972 and at *Penthouse*, the most openly erotic of the lot. Mr. Guccione, a shortish man, walked into the set wearing what looked like a badly fitting hair piece; a white lacy shirt open to the waist, exposing multiple gold chains resting on his hairy chest; tight, shiny leather pants; and black, pointy, patent-leather shoes. I was somewhat taken aback, and I stumbled through a few pleasantries before he stopped me. "Wait a minute," he said, holding his hand up like he was halting traffic, "You're not Canadian, are you?"

"No, I'm from New Jersey."

"So am I," he said.

We were off! We talked about the small seaside towns and the Jersey seashore. He knew Red Bank particularly well, where Count Basie comes from. He'd gone to tony Blair Academy, a private boy's school in northern New Jersey. I mentioned my alma mater, Miss Fine's School, and, yes, he'd gone to dances there, but after I had graduated. By now we felt like cousins. When I told him about my unsuccessful interview a few hours earlier, he laughed. "Well, you know, as they say, you win some and you lose some," he said.

Emboldened by now, my final question was, "Since we've seen Burt Reynolds and these other famous men appearing nude in print, when will we see Bob Guccione in his full glory in *Penthouse* magazine?"

"Soon," he said. "Very soon."

I'm sure he never did appear nude. He did give me a hug though, gold chains and all. The day that began with a gloomy rock star ended with some *bravissimo*.

As it turned out my foray into television interviewing – one might say mercifully – was short lived. Roberta Walker, producer of CBC Radio 740 AM's "Off-Stage Voices," a one-hour weekly arts and entertainment program left a message asking if I was interested in hosting it. I doubt that she called because she'd seen my brief appearance on television, more likely because announcers, if one could be scheduled, were not charged against a program's budget. Still, she likely knew I loved music and liked the arts. We got along well and stayed on the air from September 1974 to October 1975.

I loved working on radio, playing the music I liked and interviewing interesting people and for the most part CBC seemed to like what I was doing. Sometimes they even promoted the programs I hosted. This photograph was taken when I was hosting "Off Stage Voices" in 1975. (Photo courtesy of CBC)

In the coming months, I interviewed many fascinating performers, and I even kept a few tapes because I admired the artist so much. One of them was an interview with my favourite singer, Ella Fitzgerald, the Queen of Jazz.

Ella Fitzgerald struggled through a difficult youth in the early 1930s when she was sent to an orphanage after her mother died in an accident. Her breakthrough came in 1938, singing her own composition "A-Tisket, A-Tasket" with Chick Webb's big band. Even then, she had to contend not only with racial prejudice, but also with the prejudice she faced as a woman in the male world of jazz.

Her repertoire included mostly music from the Great American Songbook. But she could sing in any key, high or low, and couldn't be pinned down as either an alto or a high soprano. I saw her elegantly dressed in movies and television shows with Frank Sinatra, Dean Martin, Nat King Cole, Dinah Shore, and with her good friend Louis Armstrong, doing amazing, improvised scat riffs. To this day, nobody can do this as well as she did.

She came to Toronto often. On one of these occasions, October 2, 1974, the producer of our low-budget program managed to arrange a half-hour interview with her. My producer and I were both excited by the prospect. She was scheduled to sing at Toronto's famed Massey Hall that night, and I was to interview in her hotel in the morning, but when we knocked, a tired-looking older woman opened the door. A wave of eucalyptus-scented steam poured over us into the hall. The woman suggested we keep the interview short as Ella had a cold and was resting. Walking into the room was like stepping into a London fog, although it smelled sweeter. The light was dim, the window shades drawn and vaporizers on every flat surface contributed to the mist that almost concealed Ella Fitzgerald, sitting in the corner. She was propped up in an overstuffed armchair with her feet on a stool and a blanket pulled up to her neck.

She smiled warmly at us through the mist. My producer and I looked at each other, then suggested we should leave. Ella said no, we should go ahead with the interview. So we set up the mic on the table next to two cups of steaming tea and turned off the hissing vaporizers. I asked a couple of questions about her travels, which country she had liked the most (perhaps England and Germany), how she felt about Toronto, and what it was like to work with Louis Armstrong (always a welcoming surprise, she assured us). Occasionally, a question pops into an interviewer's mind and passes their lips before they realize how foolish it sounds. "Was the archbishop a religious man?" That kind of question. Mine was, "Miss Fitzgerald, how did you learn to sing?" She looked at me blankly through the lingering mist and said nothing. Finally, in her calm, even voice, she said, "Lawd child, I just open my mouth and it comes out." She went on to explain, "When I first joined Chick Webb's band in 1935, I was only sixteen. Someone suggested to Chick vocal training might be good. He said with my natural styling she didn't need a teacher. She should stay the way she sings." She went on to say she was sorry now that she never got any training, "as I hear there are some good ones."

I asked her if she was aware of just how magical her communication with her audience was. "Well, If I were aware of this, I would be self-conscious," she said. "Now I try to portray a picture or tell a story when I sing." It was her extraordinary talent for improvising that impressed so many of her fans, so I asked her how her voice could do so many maneuvers – hornlike improvisations, particularly in scat. "If I'm hoarse like right now, I try to sing around the note, sing around the melody," she said. Finally, I told her that as a student I had seen her on a tour of colleges and asked if she found touring a strain. Thirty-five weeks a year, which is what she had been doing in recent years was "more of a pleasure than work," she said.

I had a lot more questions and could easily have stayed longer, but her answers were getting shorter. It was time to leave. We thanked her for her visit, the gracious interview and wished her well for the concert that evening. I felt embarrassed. This splendid artist, feeling less than her best, had to perform in front of many hundreds of fans and I was asking her all these questions. I hoped she understood what it meant to a young woman who loved jazz to sit with her and just chat.

My interview with singer Bob Eberly, which I have also kept, was different. To start with, he was healthy when I talked with him. I was quite young when I first heard him and fell in love with his voice. I didn't know what he looked like, but he had a smooth, romantic baritone sound, which had won him a contest on Fred Allen's musical radio show in 1935. That was way before my time, but I found out about him because of a well-publicized feud between the Dorsey brothers, which ended with Tommy hiring Frank Sinatra as his star crooner and Jimmy keeping Eberly for his Orchestra. They stayed together for eight years, well into the 1950s. Jazzbo Collins occasionally played music on his late-night radio show from the 1940s big band era, even though it was going out of fashion by the mid-1950s. That's where I heard Eberly's hits "Tangerine" and "The

Breeze and I."

When my producer said we had a chance to interview Eberly, I didn't swoon because no one did that anymore, but I could have. I told her about my teenage crush, and now she too was looking forward to what might happen when we met. Unfortunately, that didn't happen. As it turned out, he was still in Ottawa doing a concert, so I didn't have a chance to meet him face to face, but over the telephone his voice sounded the same as twenty years before. He answered all my questions as if we had known each other for years.

He had toured with the band in the 1930s before he went in the army and, when he returned, worked through the 1950s. By now we were into the seventies, and I asked if he was still working full time or just occasionally. He just told me he was still really busy. I suggested that by the 1950s the big band era had pretty much come to an end. He agreed, saying that "all the adoration for Elvis and Johnny Mathis had pretty much done it in." So, I asked him what he had been doing to keep going.

"Nostalgia helps," he said. "We were relegated to small clubs, played dance halls and nightclubs like the Meadowbrook in New Jersey."

"The Meadowbrook? I grew up nearby," I said, adding, "I think that's where Sinatra started."

"That's right and people still enjoy dancing. The psychological value is good for us. Keeps us going."

He was in his sixties by then, and I said, "You don't have to do this, you know, all the hassle, travel, learning new arrangements. Why are you doing it?"

"There's a lot of ego involved," he said, laughing. "I don't get a lot of applause around the house, so I have to go amid strangers. It's really a labour of love."

It worked for me, and of course I had to ask him if he still sang any of his big hits. "I have some of your 78s," I said. But that wasn't where he wanted to go. He did offer me some advice, though: "Put heavy books on them so they don't break." I asked him about the famous ending of the 1947 version of "Green Eyes," when Helen O'Connell starts singing in double time. How did that happen?

"I'll tell you the story. We had just three minutes left to the end of a live radio show before we were off the air. We came to the last song. The arrangement had me open, Jimmy and the band come in, and then Helen ends it double time. I know the stories, but it was all planned, not an ad lib movie ending."

Before the interview ended, I asked, "Is it true you roomed with Frank Sinatra?"

"No," he laughed. "All of us singers at that time, Perry Como, my brother Ray with the Glenn Miller Band, we all ended up rooming with someone. None of us were making millions. But I didn't room with Frank Sinatra. That wouldn't have fit in with my wife."

Not wanting to be rude, but with big band music well out of favour at the time, I had to ask who was listening to him now. What kind of audiences he had. Interestingly, he said, all ages. "Older people. Young people come out, too. One little girl said to me, 'You sound like my father. You really mean what you say?' I do, of course I do."

The third interview I've kept was with Guy Lombardo, the Canadian band leader. We were coming up to Christmas holidays and we got lucky. He was coming home towards the end of December before his annual syndicated appearance on radio and television on New Year's Eve. We called him in New York, and asked whether, since he was going to be in Canada, he would like to talk to his Canadian listeners. He would be delighted. He would be in Ottawa, not Toronto, so we would have to talk by telephone. That was all right by me as he had the most pleasant, resonant voice, one that sounded like a perfect CBC announcer.

I began by telling him that to me he was a tradition like apple pie and Coca-Cola and asked how long he had been Mr. New Year's Eve. There was a long pause before he said laughingly, "Let's see, since the Depression – the 1930s – World War Two, then we switched to

TV in the 1950s for seven or eight years. I'm happy to say CBC has carried us for four or five years now." I told him that when I had lived in France, his New Year's Eve broadcast was carried on the Armed Forces Network, and it was magical. I'd feel homesick at that time every year and hearing him made me feel so much better.

Overall of those years, have you ever missed one? I asked.

"No, I hope not." He laughed again. "Touch wood, I hope I never do. I've been on the air since 1930, a couple of years after leaving London, Ontario." I asked if there was one New Year's Eve he remembered the most. "I believe when World War Two was over was the happiest time. After Pearl Harbor was probably the saddest. I think there was more fun during the Depression years as everyone was struggling in the same boat."

You're always the entertainment, I said. "Do you ever want to go to someone else's New Year's Eve party?"

"No, I've never thought of it. I like doing it. People like having fun. We're not like doctors or lawyers with problems to contend with."

He and his band had been playing for forty years by then, and tastes change, so I asked him what kind of music he was playing now. "Swing to rock-n-roll," he said. "To open, Scott Joplin music from *The Sting*, then some from the thirties, forties and fifties for the seniors and a few current songs like 'Tie a Yellow Ribbon.' The audiences all seem to like it. They're all pretty much the same over the years." He paused and laughed, "I don't mean teenagers, of course."

It was a lovely interview with a warm, charming man. At the end I said, "I've heard you do it regularly over the years, so I thought it would only be fair this year, Mr. Lombardo, for me to wish you Happy New Year." It was a good way to end the interview, and we both laughed.

In 1975, the corporation launched CBC Stereo, its second (English language) national radio network. Stereo recording was a relatively recent development, and the new service was broadcast on FM frequencies across the country, ensuring better quality reception than on the increasingly noisy AM broadcast band. It was devoted primarily to classical music, but also drama and other arts and cultural programs. The head of the music department, which was responsible for the bulk of programming on the new network, asked if I would be interested in hosting a daily ninety-minute program heard across the country between 6:30 and 8:00 p.m. "We are going to call it 'Listen to the Music,'" he said. Fredd would be the producer. Fredd and I had worked well together for the past year, and I accepted happily.

Little did Fredd and I know our on-air relationship would last for the next twelve years, through sickness and in health, ratings ups and downs, and the usual carousel of changing managers. No strangers to ham-handed program decisions, CBC managers this time chose the right producer for the program. Fredd was a small man, shy, even retiring, but with an extraordinary memory and an encyclopedic knowledge of classical music. Astonishingly, he not only knew composers and their compositions, but the number each LP had been assigned in the vast CBC music library. Fredd's programs weren't just random selections of music or simple themes like "Mozart." His scripts wove themes together and linked compositions in a storybook fashion. One day he did a program on flowers, beginning with renaissance music and ending ninety minutes later with Nat King Cole singing "Blue Gardenia." He didn't slip those pop or jazz numbers in too often, but he knew I liked them and that wouldn't really offend our loyal classical music fans.

The poster for our new classical music program, "Listen to the Music," was an irresistible attraction, at least for some. It was placed on Toronto Transit Commission subway cars, street cars and buses the week before Halloween and it seemed only a very few images of my face escaped an added mustache or black eye.

To launch the program, the publicity department put together an elegant poster with my photograph and the name and time of the program and distributed it to major cities for placement in their transit systems. In Toronto, copies were put up in subway trains. It was the nicest picture anyone ever took of me, and my name was even spelled correctly. Unfortunately, the poster went up just before Halloween, and as I rode to and from work on the subway every day, I soon noticed someone had used a thick black felt pen to add a Hitleresque moustache to my face on every poster I could see. I told Fredd I had to be careful where I sat, so I wouldn't be positioned right under one of the decorated posters. It also occurred to me that it would be worse if I sat under one and nobody recognized me, moustache or not.

We recorded our program between 5:30 and 7:00 p.m., broadcast live to Atlantic Canada 6:30 to 8:00 p.m. local time in the Maritimes (and, of course, half hour later in Newfoundland and Labrador). That first live edition to the east was rebroadcast an hour later in Toronto then "bicycled" across the country, broadcast at 6:30 p.m. local time in every western time zone.

Preparing the program each day was a lot of work, enough to my mind. But the managers scheduling the announcers overlooked that and regularly squeezed in a couple of hourly three-minute radio news broadcasts to do before my scheduled preparation time for the music show began or some other type of work in the evening after we signed off at 7:00 p.m. I still have nightmares about forgetting to pick up my schedule and missing assignments.

We had the same technician for most of the twelve years the program was on the air. He had a good ear for music and was excellent at his job. The three of us became good friends. Brian travelled regularly on the weekends and would often bring in a bottle or two of white wine for us to taste. Sipping wine in the studio was a civilized and enjoyable way to spend the afternoon. But one day we had a near disaster. Fredd knew we would be having a taste test of a new wine that day, so he programmed a very long symphony, almost all our ninety-minute program time. He had just refilled our glasses when the red light came on. I pushed the mic button and said my usual "Good evening." But, after a few sips, Brian accidentally bumped the turntable. The needle made a terrible screeching sound as it skated across the LP, a noise heard by every one of our East Coast listeners. The needle stopped about two-thirds of the way to the end of the record. I was horrified and had no idea what to do. All that careful timing out the window. We didn't have enough music to end the program, so we'd be going to dead air. We couldn't do that.

While my mind was whirling, Fredd took one look at where the needle had ended up, ran out the door without a word, down a flight of stairs to the record library in the basement of the radio building, grabbed three LPs with three pieces of music of different lengths and raced back to our studio. We had some music now, but of course we didn't know how long a piece we would need because we didn't know exactly how much had disappeared in the needle slide. We would have to be prepared to "fill" with different lengths of music to close out the show, but we would have only had seconds to decide which selection to use.

Fredd was looking noticeably ashen as he stared at the turntable. Finally, he said he thought he remembered where the slide started, and he knew where it picked up again. "I figure we've lost just about twenty minutes," he said. The technician and I looked at each other. He had to be making this up. He couldn't possibly know how much time we had to fill at the end. But he did. He selected one of the LPs, handed it to the technician and told him to cue up the third cut.

The long symphony ended twenty minutes before it was supposed to. The cut we had cued up was nineteen minutes long. Fredd gave me the information for the introduction for the new piece that would end the program. We came up to our 7:00 p.m. sign-off time. I said my usual closing: "Join us again and listen to the music." We had one minute left for the program theme music to take us out. Exactly on time. We raised our glasses to Fredd and finished our bottle of wine. Perfect. A very acceptable young vintage. But I still don't know how Fredd did it.

One summer we were asked to extend the program by an hour for a few weeks. That was when listeners were first introduced to Mme. Hortovány, a charming but rather opinionated musical savant and storyteller. Sounding remarkably like my own mother, with her thick Hungarian accent, she presented the works of lesser-known composers, adding her own often blunt evaluations. I became quite fond of her, and she was popular among our listeners. Well, maybe not all of them. My mother, who was in Toronto for a visit, heard my recording of Mme. Hortovány on the radio one evening and immediately remarked, "I don't speak that way." I didn't dare say a word.

Chapter 9

"The Kremlin's" goodbye

In late 1974, I was asked by a local TV executive whether I would be interested in anchoring CBLT's "Final Edition," the 11:00 p.m. Toronto television news. I was surprised but took it to mean that management thought it was time to show there was more than one woman staff announcer (there were then two of us. Judy Maddren was on contract) who could host a news program. Jan Tennant, who was already reading "The National," was a good friend and a fount of good advice. So I asked her opinion. She thought it was an experience that would only make me a more valuable employee.

Still, I wasn't sure. "Listen to the Music" meant a three-hour shift for me, finishing at 7:00 p.m. Anchoring "Final Edition" would mean showing up for makeup around 9:30 p.m. with sign-off at midnight. The music program was a pleasure to work on, a quiet oasis from the daily chaos and I looked forward to it every day. Live television news had frightened me since the near disaster of my first news broadcast at CBLT in 1973. "Final Edition" was broadcast once. There were no rehearsals. Whatever happened, however well or poorly things went, whatever disasters occur would be live for everyone to see. There were no teleprompters in the studio. Just like in radio, news readers read the stories typed on the script in their hands. The big difference, of course, is that it was television, and you couldn't just look down and read. You had to look at the camera and then glance down. Looking up and down like that made me afraid of losing my place, or skipping lines or re-reading them, or, worse, knocking the pages to the floor or some other foolishness happening live in front of millions of Ontario viewers. I also knew that news editors hand you the stories only minutes before airtime, so there was little time to confirm pronunciations, work through odd sentence constructions or spot unusual names or places. To be charitable, the scripts were usually late because the editors are still working on the stories. But I also knew editors who seemed to take perverse pleasure from holding back the scripts until the last few minutes to test a news reader's skill, to see if they stumbled over the unusual place names in the third or forth story.

I decided to do it anyway, thinking that if I couldn't handle the job and they fired me, I could probably work for Radio Canada, the CBC's French-language arm in Montreal. At least I had a plan.

In the end, it turned out not to be as stressful as I'd feared. Handsome young John Good was the sportscaster, and our weatherman was the splendid Bill Lawrence, who had the gift of being able to talk seamlessly for as long or as short a time as needed to end the program. These two men knew I was nervous and did their best to make me feel more in control.

Having spent most of my time on radio, I hadn't fully appreciated how television means the loss of one's anonymity. On one level it's flattering to have people you walk past on the sidewalk smile in recognition or greet you in a store and say they saw you last night on the news. But there are also some who will accost you to criticize a story or the way it was presented. One man in a supermarket walked up, looked me in the eye, and said, "I know you. You're that whore on the news." Even people you think you know can show a different side. One night around 1:00 a.m., just after I got home, a mechanic who had done some work on my old car phoned me and asked me out. When I said no, he became obscene and threatening. A woman wrote all in capital letters demanding to know why I hated the Salvation Army so much, which I do not. Another viewer sent her illustrated essay on how unflattering my hairstyle was with different drawings. Bill was sympathetic. He told me whenever his weekend weather forecast turned out to be wrong, on Monday morning he heard from angry brides whose weddings had been rained out. He advised me to get an unlisted telephone number. I did.

A big story in the news at the time was the war in Vietnam. By the spring of 1975, the Viet Cong were advancing swiftly through South Vietnam and closing in on the capital. On April 30, Saigon fell. Television stations across North America and around the world stood by for this news bulletin. As usual "The National" signed off at 10:58 p.m. There was a two-minute break before the local news went to air. Thirty seconds before the red light on the camera flashed on, the news editor dashed in and handed me the bulletin. There was no time to read the script in advance. The page shook visibly in my hand. When I got home after midnight, I discovered that, except for my face, I was covered in a red rash from all the stress. I seriously considered resigning if I couldn't be the unflappable anchor that the TV news requires. But I soon dropped that idea. The lights and the cameras still drew me like a moth to a flame.

I was now working on two programs that demanded concentration and self-control. It seems to be only when you are busy and have less time to think about yourself life presents unexpected opportunities. One early afternoon in June, I wandered into a tiny editing room near the announcer's office and my life changed for ever. Bent over an audio tape machine was a handsome young man with glorious brown hair and a beard to match.

He introduced himself as Bob Campbell, the new executive producer of "As It Happens," the legendary phone-interview program hosted by Barbara Frum on AM radio. By coincidence, it is broadcast at the same time as "Listen to the Music," my FM music program. Bob asked whether I would be interested in being the summer replacement for Al Maitland, Barbara's co-host. I declined as it would have meant giving up my music program, and besides, working on live radio: altogether more stress than I thought I could handle. I walked out of the editing room, short of breath, not because of the offer, but because of the man who made it. Who was he? Pat Wedemire the new secretary in the announce office, told me he had just returned from CBC Nova Scotia, where he produced local news programs. Then she casually pointed out there was a bright red rash on my neck.

It had been more than five years since Jean-Jacques died, and since then I had unconsciously avoided any close emotional relationships. Bob was several years younger than I am, quite a change from Jean-Jacques who was seventeen years older. But he was as struck by me as I was by him, and he asked me out. We dated three or four times, and by early September, he moved into my little house with a full toolbox, a warm but ugly winter coat, likely left over from the Korean War, and the clothes he was wearing. For the first time in years, I felt safe and happy. We have been together ever since.

Bob was truly a young man of the 1960s, a hippie who had a motorcycle, joined anti-war protests, and edited a left-wing political magazine. That's when he first let his hair and beard grow long. When he and some friends went to Woodstock in 1969, they fitted in perfectly with the muddy crowd. He never has told me what happened over those few cold days in the rain. Anyone who remembers, he says, probably wasn't there. In mid-September we took a week off and drove to Nova Scotia, beautiful at that time of year, and visited the places he loved. He was born in Toronto but went to university and worked down east. We stayed in Antigonish, a charming town where we dug for oysters on the beach. Not something a girl could do on the New Jersey seashore.

When we returned to Toronto, there was a telephone message for me to call the announce office right away. The next morning, before heading into work, we sat with a cup of coffee and looked through the newspapers that had collected on the doorstep. The warm pleasure of the early morning ended abruptly. In a mid-week paper, I found a short item at the end of the entertainment section: "Margaret Pacsu replaced as host of CBLT's 'Final Edition.'" What? I re-read it. "Replaced"? Management seemed happy when I had left a few days ago – at least as happy as they ever were with anyone's work. I'd heard no complaints. No one had spoken to me about being taken off the program. Yet shockingly, here it was, after fourteen months of reading the news, I was off the program. The three-sentence story only said I'd been replaced by a woman whose name I hadn't heard before. This was my first encounter with the ham-fisted CBC television management. As it turned out, it wouldn't be the last.

I called the announce office and was told only that I was to go to the CBLT manager's office in what we called "The Kremlin" – the mansion next to the Jarvis St. radio building.

Everyone at the CBC called it "The Kremlin," because the way management staff appeared then suddenly disappeared, and sometimes reappeared, was reminiscent of Stalinist Russia. It was a place, they said, where the rats scurry about in daytime.

I walked over and in through an open door to the manager's office. At the time, all the managers had secretaries who worked in outer offices to protect their bosses from intrusions. When I gave her my name, she knocked on an inner door and showed me inside. He stayed seated behind an oversized desk and gestured for me to sit down in a chair facing him. There was no greeting, just "Well Margaret" said with a painful sigh as if I was a misbehaving student summoned to the vice-principal's office. Then after a deep breath and glance at the corner of the ceiling, he began again. "Well Margaret, the committee feels you are not serious enough for the news." He paused to let that sink in and continued. "They feel you are probably better suited to more light-hearted television fare." He never explained what the committee was or who was on it or why it was making program decisions. He was only conveying the message, he said with a tight smile. Then stood to show the meeting was over. I left realizing I had said nothing. Anything but lighthearted, I walked out feeling bruised all over.

Chapter 10

The rinky-dink piano player

I was hurt by the way I was taken off the program, but I wasn't sorry my tenure as a news anchor had come to an end. As much as I loved being in front of the camera and the focus of attention in the studio, the aggressive and sometimes abusive treatment I got from viewers had overpowered the pleasures of the job. I had also learned that I don't have the cool nerves needed to deal with on-camera studio mishaps. It was a wonderful experience, but not one that I wanted to do for a long time. In the years since then, knowing the stress they faced daily only increased my admiration for long-time anchors Lloyd Robertson, Knowlton Nash, Peter Mansbridge, and Lisa LaFlamme. I was angry but not altogether surprised when after thirty years, Lisa was fired by Bell Media in 2022 after she stopped dyeing her by-then grey hair. In private broadcasting, upper management is still mostly male. *Plus ça change, plus c'est la meme chose....*

That was how I felt about presenting news programs, but I still enjoyed hosting other television programs, including a delightful children's quiz series called "Just for Fun," which ran for two seasons, 1975-76. The children, all seventh graders would cavort around the set, ask foolish questions, do all kinds of mildly competitive stunts such as bobbing for apples, spinning the hoop, balancing brooms. Even the crew joined in. They talked to us during the program, unheard of on live television, and the audience got to know them by name. Best of all, if they knew the answer to the question, the sound men would bob their long audio boom mics up and down and demand a prize. Those technicians, the TV and radio audio teams, the lighting crews, they were always my friends. My job was to keep the crowd of lively twelve-year-olds from getting out of hand. "Just for Fun" aired on Tuesdays at 5:00 p.m., when our young school crowd was at home. I hosted the program for a year, and then I got in an internal mail envelope stuck in my pigeonhole in the announce office saying they didn't need me on the program anymore, thank you. I had been replaced midway through its second season in 1976. There was no reason, no explanation. Not even done in person. The fun was over. I had a much harder time forgiving CBC managers for this one. It was no consolation when the show was cancelled altogether after the season ended.

But staff announcers present programs and are there to be assigned at whim. I often thought producers looked at the announce pool much the way I would pick out a lively looking lobster in a store's tank. "That one. No. The one in the corner, there." That's likely how I was chosen, along with Radio Canada announcer Henri Bergeron, to present the Prix Anik Awards program, annual awards given for excellence in various areas of both CBC and Radio-Canada. Awards programs make everyone feel happy, and M. Bergeron was a delight to work with.

Less understandable was being sent to Moscow. In the early 1970s, Cold War tensions were easing somewhat. Leonid Brezhnev, general secretary of the Communist Party, had made some political and economic reforms and the Iron Curtain lifted a little, just enough for a cultural exchange: A popular Russian state television program would come to film in Canada and CBC would go to Moscow.

In their usual mysterious fashion, CBC managers chose me to go. I have no idea why and no one told me. But in early February 1976, three of us, all immigrants– an excellent camera operator from Ceylon, a producer from Britain, and me from New Jersey but with a

Hungarian surname – flew out of Montreal to represent Canada in the cold and dark of mid-winter Moscow. It had not escaped our attention that this was not a choice assignment, and we all searched our pasts at CBC for what we could have done to warrant being chosen. We were to film "Margaret in Moscow", as a special program. Happy to benefit from any warm feelings that might result from this rare Cold War thaw, the federal government and CBC publicized the initiative, which led much of the press and the public to assume the Margaret was Margaret Trudeau, the prime minister's wife, who was in the news at the time for dancing at New York's Studio 54.

Bob was not happy I would be away for two weeks in the coldest part of winter. Expecting that phoning him from Moscow would be impossible, I promised to send postcards and letters. I did send them, all worded cryptically, le Carré style, but he never received them. The Air Canada flight to London was pleasantly uneventful and largely silent. The three of us attempted casual conversation without success because we were nervous at the prospect of living and working together for two weeks in an enemy country. The Aeroflot flight to Moscow was as grim as our mood was by then, but the cameraman entertained me with stories about some of the interesting places he had been. My producer said nothing. He struck me as a loner and perhaps disappointed we were not doing an exposé of the failure of communism. I didn't think he much liked my friendly, concerned interviewing manner, so I judged it best not to speak much, and we didn't.

Things began to look up a bit when we landed at Sheremetyevo. A tall, handsome young Russian in a black Cossack fur hat named Kyril Morganov greeted us with a broad smile at the exit gate after we had navigated a line of po-faced customs and police officers. He spoke good English, and immediately asked where the rest of my crew was. He looked stunned when we told him there were just the three of us and said, "Just two-and-a-half weeks ago, your Mary

Tyler Moore was here filming a celebration of the two-hundredth anniversary of the Bolshoi Theatre. They had six camera operators, at least twenty crew members, make-up, and costume assistants. They filmed the *Romeo and Juliet* ballet, with the orchestra playing Prokofiev's music. Famous ballerinas performed the principal roles."

We clarified we were from Canada, that Mary Tyler Moore was an American show, and that we were planning to use excerpts from lighthearted Soviet programs – quiz programs, variety shows, nothing political, and nothing like the Bolshoi Ballet. All would be original Russian tape except for occasional short live links, as we called them, which we would film for our Canadian viewers. Ivan said nothing about our aims, but explained he would accompany us all the time, "to help confirm film locations and solve any bureaucratic obstacles." Who did we want to film, and did we want to film anywhere prohibited? He was just there to make our job easier, he said. He didn't mention he would be keeping an eye on us as well.

He drove us to a Stalinist, wedding-cake-style hotel, with ironclad rules for foreign guests that made settling into our accommodations somewhat disconcerting. On each floor, a large and sinister-looking woman sat on the landing with a clear view of the hallway. The woman on our floor handed each of us the key to our room. Ivan explained that whenever we left the room, we had to return the key to her. No nonsense here and full knowledge of our movements. I soon found out that similar overweight, menacing women sat at the doors to GUM, the famous Moscow department store. When I went, the woman I encountered demanded that I leave my bag at the door and account for everything I bought. However, there was nothing to buy – the shelves were mostly empty – so I escaped without having to communicate at length.

As to the food, the hotel menu was not exactly gourmet. The eggs were undercooked every morning, the dark brown flour used in the bread was from Canada they told us proudly. The borscht at noon tasted as good as I imagined, but it was the only dish on offer and there never was any other choice. There was no wine but lots of vodka served in shot glasses. The Russians drank multiple shots, each in one gulp, quickly followed by the next. The object seemed to get drunk as fast as possible. They looked at us oddly as we sipped our glassfuls.

Also, there were never any vegetables or fruit, except the cabbage in the borscht, and by the end of two weeks I was in digestive trouble. One day, the Canadian ambassador invited us to lunch at the embassy, a lovely house with a thatched roof in the middle of the city. It was so good to eat a Canadian meal with salad and apples and to speak without translation with the ambassador and his assistant. As the meal and the wines progressed, I began asking about Soviet politics and jokingly queried whether the dining room was bugged. No one answered, and I immediately realized how naïve my question was. After the maid serving us left the room, the ambassador put his finger to his lips. "Les murs ont des oreilles. The walls have ears," he whispered. I'd seen that phase written everywhere in Paris in May 1968. I felt uneasy and foolish at not being more cautious.

It was dark in Moscow after about 6:30 p.m. There were few streetlights, no shops with illuminated windows, no publicity signs, and only a few pedestrians on the sidewalks, all dressed in dark clothes. No one looked at us, despite our camera equipment. When they saw Kyril with us, they usually turned away.

I'm not the first one to discover that winter is not the best time to visit Moscow. In February 1976, the CBC sent me to the Soviet capital to shoot "Margaret in Moscow." Standing in the square in front of Lenin's tomb something less than a smile was about all I could manage. (Photo courtesy of CBC).

One morning we were filming the sights in Red Square – the wonderful St. Basil Cathedral with its nine vibrantly coloured cupolas, Lenin's Tomb, and The Kremlin. Groups of tourists were strolling around, some with guides. A few stopped to watch what we were doing and to listen to us speaking English. One young couple asked where in the States we come from. We're from Toronto, Canada, we explained. Oh, they said and hurried off, looking disappointed. No Muscovite ever asked us what we thought of their city or even gave us a smile in passing. It was as if we didn't exist. We soon learned not to take it personally. They acted that way with each other as well. We finished filming in Red Square. It took me five attempts to get it right because the producer changed the script after each take, making it hard for me to remember what he wanted. At one point, to steal a few moments of quiet for myself, I walked around a corner of a huge building, most likely part of The Kremlin, and was startled to come face-to-face with a squad of soldiers in dress uniform brandishing sub-machine guns. They looked at me and rushed forward yelling loudly in Russian and waving their weapons. I quickly turned back to rejoin Kyril and my crew of two. I was really frightened. What if they had arrested me and spirited me away to some frozen gulag never to see anyone I love again? Why had I come on this trip anyway? I felt stupid for always being so pleased to be asked, always saying yes. Kyril was upset and told me angrily under no circumstances to stray off again. He was responsible for me, for the three of us, so I shouldn't make trouble for him. I never wandered off again, but that day I wanted to run away from Russia entirely.

Filming "Margaret in Moscow" proved to be complicated. The producer only ever handed me the on-camera links just before shooting the scenes and expected me to know them by heart. It was the same problem I had reading live TV news. Under pressure I could not remember texts I'd barely had time to read. So, I had to do numerous takes. Neither the cameraman nor the producer was pleased. The mood turned gloomy, exacerbated by a drop in the temperature, and progress slowed. A Russian make-up artist joined us for exterior shots. She was a sweet young woman who never complained about standing in the bitter cold in only a thin cloth coat. It quickly became clear that she didn't really have any make up, so we used what little I'd brought from Canada. Before filming, she did my hair in her tiny office in the Ostankino TV tower, then the tallest freestanding structure in Europe. Her equipment consisted of a tiny charcoal stove topped with a grill, which she used to heat up long curling irons that looked like medieval weapons. She did her best, but the room soon smelled of burning hair – mine.

That week, the temperature fell to a new low, dropping to minus thirty Celsius. Our cameraman's equipment froze, and he developed a high fever. He ended up in a British medical clinic for a short stay, and they wouldn't allow any visitors. The cold didn't seem to matter to the many Muscovites, men and women, we saw breaking the ice and jumping half-naked into one of the city's many outdoor swimming pools to refresh themselves in the freezing water.

One day, our assignment from Soviet TV was to watch a program hosted by their principal variety star. We hoped to select excerpts from her six-hour show. When we got to the studio theatre, we were told an audience was about to arrive to provide enthusiastic support. We huddled in a dark corner awaiting the crowd, and eventually the doors opened. Some three hundred noticeably short men in military uniforms marched in silently and filled up the seats. They looked as if they were all from a far-flung Asiatic corner of the U.S.S.R. There were no flashing light cues for audience applause or laughter. The program rolled along with music, interviews, and commentary but without any response from the audience. We had no idea what was being said but enjoyed being in such a wonderfully warm space. About one hour into the program, we noticed an odd droning sound, as if a swarm of bees had settled down around us. The soldiers were all sound asleep – eyes closed, heads bowed, and gently snoring in a synchronized rhythm. It may have been the first time in months they found themselves in a safe, warm place. They looked so peaceful and so young.

Making "Margaret in Moscow" was not exactly an ordeal but it was demanding, nevertheless. We managed to finish on schedule, despite the cameraman's illness and the freezing weather. The lasting impression I have of the city is of a quiet, dull place, whose citizens lived in Stalinist style high-rises and seemed always aware of eyes watching them. A sad city. Even the Red Army Chorus, famous for its powerful male voices, seemed to sing only in sad, minor keys. I bought their latest album for Fredd. I was sure he'd appreciate it. The three of us got ready to leave. The producer and cameraman packed up their gear, said goodbye, and caught the first plane back to London. My plan was to visit the renowned collection of French impressionist paintings in the Hermitage Museum in Leningrad (now St. Petersburg, its original name).

I told only the airline ticket and hotel reservation agents about my change of plan and took a local flight. As soon as I walked into the terminal in Leningrad, a young woman approached me, saying in perfect French, "Mlle. Pacsu, I am here to accompany you to your hotel." I asked her how she knew I was on that flight from Moscow. "Oh," she said, smiling, "we always know."

My hotel was named the Evropeyskaya during the Soviet period and dates from 1875. It is known now as the Hotel Europa. When I stayed there it looked and felt like any elegant older hotel in Paris. The main entrance was covered in faded red velvet, the brass fittings were tarnished, but the bathtub in my room was enormous. I loved the place. Best of all everyone except for a few guests spoke French.

The Hermitage Museum is immense. Catherine the Great helped herself to treasures from everywhere and founded the museum as a private gallery for her collection. There was a lot more to see than Impressionist masterpieces, but I was there only for those works of art and walked past case after case of ornate silver items.

The collection overwhelmed me. It includes works by the painters I was familiar with, including Matisse and my beloved Cezanne, but also many unknown to me. After almost four hours immersed in a surrounding of shimmering colour, I came upon a modest bookstand. The saleswoman asked me, in French of course, where I was from, did I have western currency, what kind of book was I interested in? She picked up a sizable volume in French, just published in 1975, which included accurate colour photographs of the entire paintings. Only foreigners with foreign currency could buy the book. I didn't ask her why it wasn't available to everyone, I was just grateful she wanted to sell it to me. This book was the only important souvenir I bought, even though it was costly. I have treasured it for decades.

A group of young Russians saw me sitting on a bench looking at the photographs. They came over and asked politely in French if they could look through the pages with me as they couldn't buy the book. They were like classmates. We each picked out our favorite paintings and spent quite a while discussing them. No one bothered us. Of course, they wanted to know about life in Canada, why I was in the

Soviet Union, and what Canadians thought of Russians. It felt odd sitting and talking with a group of strangers, particularly Russians. It was like being with a group of distant cousins I'd never met before. They were charming people. We were reluctant to say goodbye, but eventually they wished me *bon voyage* and went their way. I doubted that such an encounter would have been allowed in Moscow.

French was a common language among the upper class in nineteenth-century Russia, and this city still retained a European atmosphere. I'd felt so lonely in Moscow, but in Leningrad people smiled at me, and when I asked for directions, they answered in beautiful French. The city reminded me of an old French town caught in a time warp.

While I was in the hotel dining room enjoying a gourmet breakfast, a change from Moscow, an overweight middle-aged man who had been eating alone walked over and introduced himself. He told me he was a Harvard professor. He asked my name and said that we had met many years ago in Boston. Did I remember him? Eventually, I thought I did, although it seemed strange to meet anyone here from so long ago. He sat down and after chatting for ten minutes, he said he had a favour to ask, and could we go for a walk along the Nevsky Prospect, the crowded main street in front of the hotel. Reluctantly, I agreed. At first we chatted and contemplated the busy passing scene, but after a while he glanced about nervously and said he had some notes he was afraid would be confiscated at the airport. "What kind of notes?" I asked. Just lecture notes from his courses, he said. But because he was Jewish, he would attract the attention of Russian customs officials. No one would ever look for documents in my handbag. I hesitated, but he persisted. Finally, I agreed. I had always wanted to play the part of an Eastern European spy in a film noir, and this was close. He handed me the newspaper he was carrying and said the notes were in a self-addressed envelope inside it. We walked back to the hotel talking casually about the old days in Boston. I never heard from him again. I never found out what the lecture notes were about, and no one paid me any attention clearing Soviet customs. Back in Toronto, I bought stamps and dropped the envelope in a mailbox. It was addressed to an initialed company in Cambridge, Massachusetts. Bob told me later what a risky thing this was to do. For all I knew, the notes could have concealed microdots of plans for rocket engines. I never did learn what it was all about.

The overnight train back to Moscow was old and noisy, and the lone first-class car was shabby, its windows covered with grime, the little toilet and sink caked with filth. There was no running water. Overweight and ill-natured female conductors sat at each end of the car to prevent anyone from the second-class from getting in. The women were each making tea in a samovar set over little coal-burning stoves. I had a berth but couldn't sleep because of the clatter of the train, the sound of footsteps pacing back and forth in the corridor, and voices speaking loudly in Russian outside my compartment. Finally, the train arrived in Moscow, and I managed to make my way to Sheremetyevo airport. The police and customs officers paid me little attention and I joined the lineup to board an Aeroflot Ilyushin 62 to London.

I was starting to think I might be allowed to leave without a bureaucratic confrontation when Kyril appeared. He was bringing me a goodbye present of two books – one was a colourful collection of violent war posters picturing Russia defeating Germany in the Second World War. The other was all caricatures of the Fuhrer in defeat. Ivan gave them to me with evident pride, saying he wished I could stay but knowing it was impossible. He dreams of visiting the West one day, and then he will come to see me. He thinks I am very brave to come to the Soviet Union. Then he reached down, enfolded me in a bear hug and kissed me. Not a brotherly kiss but a fervent embrace. I hadn't realized when he scolded me for straying off in Red Square that he'd been worried about me, not just about how his own competence would be perceived by his bosses. I burst into tears, which made saying goodbye more difficult. I couldn't express my emotional confusion. This young man was trapped in the U.S.S.R, and I was about to walk through the open gate to the West. Then abruptly all of us in line were herded down the corridor to the plane. I looked back, he waved then disappeared in the crowd. It felt as if the Iron Curtain was clanging shut.

The flight was uneventful but when I arrived at Heathrow, the tears flowed again, and the pretty Air Canada ticket agent handed me a Kleenex. "You must have come from the Soviet Union," she said. "Don't worry. You'll be home soon." Bob was there to meet me when I arrived in Toronto. I was so relieved. Everything looked bright in the snow, with streetlights and the store windows all lit up, the sidewalks filled with well-dressed, cheerful shoppers. On the way home, we stopped at the grocery story to buy vegetables and fresh fruit, all readily available in mid-February. *Dosvidaniya*, goodbye to Russia.

I felt so anxious, I couldn't sleep. The fruit and beautiful green vegetables didn't appeal to me. Even in the daytime, I was getting flashes of the bleak streets of Moscow and the dour faces that stared at me are there. I was trapped by Moscow's dark, oppressive atmosphere. Nowadays we call this post traumatic stress disorder. Our cheery little house failed to comfort me, and despite Bob listening endlessly to my babble and asking questions to help me express my fears, nothing seemed to help. When I returned to CBC and the familiar shabby announce office, everyone welcomed me back and asked how my trip was. I barely know what to say. On top of my distress, I was feeling dizzy and feverish. I was scheduled to do a radio interview with British maestro Neville Marriner, conductor of the Academy of St. Martin in the Fields. He was an approachable man, and we chatted about British composers, his orchestra, and other similar ones. I enjoyed talking to him. When I returned to the announce office to catch my breath, one of the announcers noticed I look pale, and asked if I knew my eyes were yellow. No, I didn't. I looked in the mirror. Yep, they're yellow.

I called my doctor who told me to get to his office that afternoon.

The diagnosis didn't take him long. "You have hepatitis, my dear," he said. "Go home and stay in bed." Then he added, "And it's highly contagious." I asked about Bob. "Tell him to come down in for a gamma globulin shot." I did. But on my way home I thought about Maestro Marriner. I phoned the announce office, and they called him in California to let him know his CBC interviewer was contagious and advised him to get a gamma globulin shot.

It was a case of *From Russia with Love*. I don't know where I picked it up, but I always suspected that dirty first-class coach on the train from Leningrad to Moscow. I was seriously ill. Ten minutes out of bed and I was exhausted, and the extra pounds I usually found hard to lose just slid away. It was weeks before I could climb the stairs up to Fredd's office on the third floor of the radio building. Small to begin with, it was usually crowded with LPs, stacks of books, and papers spilling off his desk onto the floor. There was just enough room for a second chair for me while we planned that day's program. By the time I returned to work, the office was impenetrable. The piles of records, books about composers and junk that he would never let me throw out now buried my chair too. Still, it was so good to be back. In Russia I'd had been either unable to sleep or depressed. But now I had stretches when I felt just fine, although they never lasted. These mood swings were beginning to bother me.

One steamy July afternoon while walking up the half dozen, worn, black metal stairs into the radio building, I almost bumped into an odd-looking man talking to Tom, one of our radio technicians. He quickly backed away. I looked at him and he looked at me. Tom, who has a thick Scottish accent, said, "Margaret, you know Glenn? Glenn, you know Margaret?" Glenn replied, "Yes, yes, we know each other," and quickly turned away. That was all. I'd never met him before and didn't know him at all, although I knew about him, of course. And there he was. It was very hot that day and Glenn was wearing a heavy wool overcoat, beret, and fingerless gloves. I didn't notice his shoes, but he certainly appeared exactly like he did in the photos on his latest album, except he wasn't sitting on a sawed-off piano bench.

"Margaret in Moscow" aired in mid-July 1976 and garnered positive reviews in the press, not so much for my role but because of the glimpse it gave viewers of Soviet culture. The Russian program excerpts we'd included looked quite different from western television programming, even the colour of the film was unusual. I received a positive note from Knowlton Nash, director of television information programing. He wrote: "I am pleased to find out from the summer BBM ratings [Bureau of Broadcast Measurements], and I think you will be too, that "Margaret in Moscow" got an audience of just under one million, a rather substantial audience for this time of year. Audience size was recorded at 949,000. That puts it at #8 on the audience Hit Parade for Canadian shows on CBC for all viewers aged 2 and up. The program was for instance, behind such shows as 'The National', football and 'The Irish Rovers.' In any event, it was a well watched program and one of the top ten for us in the summer." What a pleasure to receive such a nice note from a television manager –the first and only time it ever happened.

Unfortunately, and I shouldn't have been surprised by it, there was a downside – the hate mail. It took much more effort to express your views back then because it required a pen or crayons, paper, an envelope, a stamp, and a walk to the post box. Nevertheless, I received newspaper clippings with my photo defaced by scrawled remarks implying I was a communist, a red, a traitor who should go back where I came from. Those were just the politically inclined. What I did enjoy was getting cheerful letters from the late poet, painter, and musician Mendelson Joe.

On one of those warm days in July, Fredd and I were in his office after our nightly recording of "Listen to the Music," when Glenn appeared. I knew he had an office on the same floor – more like a closet – it was hard to keep that a secret in the music department. But because he usually came in late in the day after everyone had gone home, no one had ever seen him there. This was only the second time

I'd noticed him in the radio building, and perhaps after our first meeting by the door he felt he knew me well enough not to say hello or introduce himself. He just stood there slightly stooped, still in his overcoat, and started asking questions about obscure musicians. Fredd knew enough answers to maintain his credibility as a music producer and to satisfy Glenn, who went back to his office. We didn't yet know that he loved to play games, but from then on, every few days we would find a musical quiz waiting for us when we came into the office. The questions weren't easy. And there was no Google to find the answer. On different days he asked who were Gertrude Kolisch, Lou Andreas-Salome, and Pauline de Ahna? Who had ever heard of these women? Fredd often knew the answers, but Glenn was gleeful any time he stumped us. And he did on Gertrude Kolisch. She was Arnold Schoenberg's wife. And Lou Andreas-Salome? She was Freud's lover. German soprano Pauline de Ahna was married to Richard Strauss. These early lighthearted meetings probably set the tone for my future relationship with Glenn. I didn't expect anything from him and was always aware of his fragile psyche. But we became an off-the-map oasis for him. Of course, he had to be the quizmaster controlling the games, but we were happy to let him.

Chapter 11

How to make a house haunted

One evening while I was in Moscow, Bob was climbing the stairs in our little house when they pulled loose. As is common enough in Toronto, the previous owner had taken down walls without regard to what they were supporting. Another time he discovered a live electrical wire on the floor under the bathtub. Someone had replaced some but not all, of the old knob and tube wiring. Bob had fixed leaks in the roof in the winter and put in new supports for the porch in the summer. He repaired the things we knew about and found many more. The house was now in good condition, and I was afraid he would get bored without another home reno to challenge him, as if being executive producer of "As It Happens" wasn't enough. So, we started biking around the neighborhood which we liked very much, with an eye out for houses for sale. We did visit a few not far from where we lived, but most of them did not appeal to us. Either they were too big or too small or badly repaired or not repaired at all.

But there was one house, not for sale, that did appeal. Older than all the rest, it was built of yellow bricks now stained with age. It had tall chimneys and a wide veranda with a roof supported by four round columns painted yellow and trimmed with green. It sat on a hill and had a stately old-fashioned air to it, with just a tinge of spookiness that on a dark fall night was hard to miss. Although it needed paint and looked to be in mild disrepair, we fell for the place, loved its gracefulness, and some evenings would bike over just to admire it. One evening, we rode past and saw a tall white-haired man raking up a mountain of leaves on the sloping lawn. It was the first time we had seen anyone around the house, and the last. We biked past it many more times but never saw him again.

One gloomy late November afternoon, I stopped at a neighborhood antique store on my way home and found an elegant nineteenth-century bayonet, almost two feet long. A small white tag tied to the handle said 1881, the date stamped on the blade, and the price. Bob was a student of that period of military history, so I bought it for him.

We had ridden past the house again the night before and once again speculated about who lived in it and what it might look like inside. This time, I thought we'd done enough speculating. If I had the courage to read the television news live to millions (well almost), surely, I could muster up enough to walk up the stairs and knock on the door, ask a couple of questions, and end our curiosity about who lived there. After all, I was well dressed, if still rather heavily made up from television, and I was not distributing detergent samples like I did for Burke years ago. This should be a piece of cake, I told myself as I walked up to the door, entirely forgetting that I was carrying a long bayonet in a polished scabbard.

I stood on the porch for a minute to catch my breath and knocked on the green half glass double-doors. No answer. The house was dark. I knocked again, a little harder this time. This time I saw a dim light come on somewhere in the back of the house and then a cheerful looking elderly woman opened the door. "Yes," she said, "May I help you?"

I stood on the porch in the gathering gloom, bayonet in hand, and told her we had admired her house for a long time and wondered if she had ever considered selling it. She didn't answer but looked me up and down, noticed the date on the white tag hanging from the bayonet, smiled, and said, "You know the house was built 1881." She paused and then asked if we would like to come for tea at four the following Saturday afternoon to meet her husband. "Yes," I said, "We would like that very much."

That Saturday afternoon was gloomy and threatening rain. At 4:00 p.m. we knocked on the door. The house was as dark as it had been when I had introduced myself. No answer. We tried again, hoping they hadn't forgotten or changed their minds. This time, the woman opened the door and invited us into the parlour to meet her husband, who had been sitting in a chair by the fire. He was a tall man, thin with white hair and wearing a blue blazer with a military crest on the breast pocket, a shirt and tie, and creased grey slacks. Clearly, he had dressed for the occasion which made us both happy that we too had dressed to meet them.

She brought in a tray with a teapot and cups and saucers and then a plate of small sandwiches on crustless white bread and oatmeal cookies that looked homemade. We told them where we worked and something of our backgrounds. He said he was a doctor and had served overseas with the Canadians. We assumed he was talking about the Second World War, until he said he had worked as an orthopedic surgeon and had been at Vimy Ridge. After the war, he had treated veterans and eventually set up a private practice that he ran for many years out of the house. His wife was among the first group of nurses to graduate from the University of Toronto. That was in 1915. She explained the house was her family's and she had grown up there.

After tea, she asked us if we would like to see the building. A brief tour started with climbing a set of back stairs to the third floor. It was getting dark by then and as we went into each room, she turned on a dim ceiling light and then turned it off as we left. We went in and out of rooms and along dark hallways on one floor and then another, finally walking down the wide front stairs through the front hall and back to the parlour where the doctor had dozed off by the fire.

They said they had thought about selling the house and they had had some offers recently but had turned them down. All were from developers whose thinly veiled intentions were to knock the house down and the neighbours' as well, replacing them with a high-rise apartment building. They didn't want to see it torn down, but they knew they couldn't stay forever and were planning to move to a seniors' residence as soon as there was room.

They were a charming couple, interesting, funny and a joy to talk with, and were not surprised when we said we loved the house and were interested in buying it and could only imagine how attached they were to it. We made an offer, then in a moment of inspiration, said that if we did buy it, they would be welcome to live in it as long as they wanted. We had no children or pets, and we could live on the third floor, and they could stay where they were. They didn't say anything, but we talked a little more, shook hands, and thanked them for the tea. As we were leaving, she asked if we would come back next Saturday to meet their son. Of course, we would.

As we walked home, we realized two things: We couldn't recall our tour of the house well enough to make a floor plan, and because we'd only been given a dimly lit glimpse, we hadn't the slightest idea of what any of the rooms looked like, except for the parlour. That took on greater weight as it slowly dawned on us that, when we shook hands as we left, we had bought the house. We did meet them again the following week with their son and to our amazement, they agreed to our unusual offer. Perhaps appropriately we moved in on April 1, 1977.

That first night in our new home, we went for a walk around the neighborhood to take in the new view, returning around 10:00 p.m. only to find the front door locked and chained. The neighbours welcomed us in and invited us to call the doctor. It took only one ring to awaken him, and he hurried down to unlock the door. He had chained it every night for four decades, and he was apologetic for his forgetfulness. We spent five months together and we enjoyed every minute of it. It was a special relationship. I never knew my grandparents, but the doctor and his wife came close to being mine.

The doctor practised medicine until 1977, when he and his wife moved out, leaving behind almost everything that they and their family had not wanted. The room where he examined patients was filled with test tubes, vials, and boxes of pills which we had to dispose of carefully. His wife left cookbooks from the twenties and thirties and a little brown box of index cards containing her most precious recipes. I have been making her oatmeal cookies, the same kind we had the first time we met them, for over forty-five years. We also inherited scores of antique books, some paintings, a large RCA Victor radio-record player that still works, the stubby remains of sixteen corn brooms (potential tomato stakes), a substantial amount of coal, which we were going to get rid of until we realized all the fireplaces burned coal.

At last, there would be space for all my records, classical and jazz in the living room and I bought a small studio piano. I'm not a good pianist, but I can stumble through some of the classics in the American Song Book. One day early in our stay, Bob discovered a treasure trove of shutters shoved into the crawl space under the porch. The newspapers folded up with them dated from the fall of 1941. Over time he has restored the shutters. We also discovered there was gas piping for lights throughout the house, and for a while we thought it would be charming to get the system working again. When we called the insurance company to double check, they told us it was against the law to have working gas circuits and that our home insurance would be cancelled immediately if we used it. We abandoned that idea.

We thought we were alone in the house, but we soon began to hear noises from the third floor, particularly the sound of furniture scraping across the floor. The doctor and his wife had mentioned a grey lady who they'd been told inhabited the third floor but if she existed, she was harmless, they said. We had moved down to the second-floor master bedroom by then. One night we had been looking at some old deeds and documents about the property. We turned off the light and shortly afterward the large, cast brass reading lamp next to Bob's side of the bed, snapped and fell over on his head. Some time later, when I was out and he was working in the basement, he heard footsteps on the kitchen floor directly above him. He called out and when I didn't answer, came upstairs to see who it was. There was no one there. It was not the only time we heard footsteps in the kitchen when there was no one there to make them.

And it wasn't just us. A few years ago, a real estate saleswoman and her partner persuaded me to let them visit the house. They had a look around and were about to leave. The woman was standing with me by the radiator in the front hall asking about our intentions to sell the property. We had none, I assured her. Suddenly, she fell over. She didn't trip, she fell as if she'd been pushed. She stared at me accusingly for a moment but saw that I was too far away. I helped her up and they left, not a little shaken. Bob and I were sceptical about these occurrences, and always tried to explain them away, but they were unnerving nonetheless.

One summer afternoon I was sitting on the porch reading when a pleasant-looking woman came up the steps and asked for the doctor and his wife. I told her they'd died a few years ago. We began talking and she said that when she was a student nurse, she and two of her classmates had rented the third floor when the doctor and his family were away for two months. They hadn't lived there long when one of them said she had to leave. She had been there alone the previous night and had heard noises that frightened her. She wasn't going to risk being that scared again. This happened to the second nurse as well, but she also heard the noises in the daytime. The woman telling me the story was the only one left. She was getting ready to go to a dance when she heard furniture moving around in the kitchen on the third floor. Terrified, she ran downstairs just as her boyfriend, a doctor, walked in. She wouldn't stay there a minute longer, she said, and waited downstairs while he ran up to find out what was going on. A few minutes later he came racing down the stairs white as a sheet, she said, saying he thought the noise might be squirrels, but it sounded like someone crying. They both left the house immediately and she only came back to pack her clothes.

I told the nurse we had heard some odd noises but never crying. We did have one other odd experience, though. In 1999, *Goosebumps*, a television series for teenagers, asked to use our house as the location for an episode called "The House of No Return." I had worked with Sherry Wolfson, the production manager, on a commercial so she was aware we were in broadcasting and thought we would be more understanding of the production process than most. The episode was set in the nineteenth century and told the story of a couple who trap evil boys who break into an old, scary house and keep them there forever. A nice boy comes looking for them and manages to escape from the creepy place.

At the time our house was well over a hundred years old, but after Goosebumps *turned it into the star of "The House of No Return" it looked much older and a lot more dilapidated than it was.*

The production team turned our house into a decrepit old building with boarded up windows, broken shutters, dead bushes all around the porch, an old iron gate at the bottom of the hill with vicious concrete eagles on top. Inside they filmed electronic bats flying around the downstairs and played scary noises for the soundtrack. It was quite a production. We spent the duration in a fancy hotel at their expense. We were assured filming would only take five days to film, but it took ten. On the last night, we went by to see what was happening. The director was sitting in the mobile unit outside watching the video feeds. The cameramen and crew were trying to wrap up the last interior scene in the front hall. It was dusk.

Then we heard the raised voice of the director in the trailer. "Tell that woman to get off the set." There was a pause. "The grey-haired woman, tell her to get out of my shot." Pause again. He was talking to the floor director in the house, "What do you mean you don't see her? She's standing by the door. The old woman. Tell her to move." Everything stopped. The floor director couldn't see anything. The camera crew was puzzled, the director was insistent. But after a few minutes, he thanked everyone and said, "All clear now. Let's finish up and get out of here." This episode was one of the most memorable in the series for both viewers and the crew. It was a success, but the director was unnerved enough to vow never to come near the house again.

In June 1981, the hundredth anniversary of the house, Bob and I decided to get married. We had made it through five years together and thought it was time to make our relationship formal. We invited Jan Tennant and her partner George Robertson, over for drinks on the porch to let them know. We expected congratulations and good wishes, but they stayed silent after we told them. Then Jan asked why we were doing this. At first, we didn't know what to say. We knew

Jan and George had been together for many years but had never married. We changed the subject, but we wanted a family and felt – at that time – it might be awkward for our children if their parents weren't married.

We were married at Toronto old City Hall on June 24, 1981, by a Justice of the Peace who wore an elegant turban and pronounced my name perfectly. On July 5, a beautiful summer day, we held a reception on our sloped front lawn. In recognition of the hundredth anniversary of the house, we asked our thirty-or-so guests and family to dress in Victorian costumes, and they all did, except for my mother who wore a tailored suit. The ladies wore colourful gowns with large multicolored feathered hats and gloves. The gentlemen sported morning suits with the odd one in a frock coat and a top hat. Bob's parents looked splendid in their period finery. Malabar, the supplier of theatrical costumes, must have done well that day. Bob looked happy and so handsome in an elegant grey suit, high starched collar, and ascot, especially with his beard, which was all the fashion in the 1880s. My wedding dress was perfect. Bob had noticed it on display in our nearby antique store, Robinson's, where I had found his bayonet. The dress dated from 1882, cost $200, and had been in the store window for weeks as there was no demand for antique wedding dresses. It made me so happy to wear a real costume and be surrounded by friends who participated in our fantasy.

We were married in July 1981, exactly one hundred years after the last bricks were laid in the old house we bought, and in an inspired moment we thought dressing up would be good way to celebrate that anniversary.

The afternoon was magical, a performance to remember. On the porch a harpist played a variety of melodies, classical and popular. A wedding buffet, including a cake in the shape of a Victorian house was the centrepiece on the porch table. Around mid-afternoon Judy Maddren's husband, Timothy Elliot, dressed in a Victorian minister's outfit asked Bob and I to kneel on the porch steps while he read the blessing. As the afternoon light began to fail, the scene took on an authentic Victorian feeling. For a little while at least there was an air of enchantment about the occasion. I was also truly amazed to be getting married at the age of forty-three. With Jean-Jacques, whom I loved so much, the idea of such a commitment had terrified me. This time there was no trauma, no uncertainly, no doubts. Ever since Bob and I first met, we have known as the poet says we were made for each other.

Charlotte Cook, my maid of honour and best friend, at my wedding.

Chapter 12

Márta meets Glenn

I now often run into Glenn Gould in the parking lot outside the Jarvis Street building, and up in the music department on the third floor. Once in the cramped basement cafeteria, his Scottish technician spotted him and yelled out across all the tables, "There goes the rinky-dink piano player." We all laughed except for Glenn, who had little sense of humour, and none about himself.

In 1977, CBC management persuaded him to host "Arts National," the network's prestigious arts and music radio show, for a whole week. He agreed on the condition he could do whatever he wanted on the final afternoon. I was told management was apprehensive he would do something far too eccentric, but the prospect of one of the country's premier musicians hosting the program outweighed their concern, and he got the go-ahead. Soon afterward Glenn dropped into our small "Listen to the Music" office – more accurately, he stood outside it because there was no room to come in – and asked me to be the straight man in what turned out to be the Friday program. I was delighted he wanted to work with me and accepted with real pleasure. It was for a role in his sketch "Memories of Maude Harbour." Moments before we started recording the segment in Studio D, just around the corner from the rather tawdry ground-floor men's room, Glenn excused himself. I waited. The technician waited. When he came back his hands were bright red. He noticed my curious glance and explained a trifle sheepishly that he always soaked his hands in hot water before a performance. I blurted out, "But this isn't a piano performance. We can redo it or fix any errors we need to." Glenn thought about it for a moment and replied, "I suppose it is mildly neurotic, isn't it?" For one of the few times in my life, I said absolutely nothing. We recorded the script in one take. Glenn seemed pleased with the result.

I never fully understood the sketch, nor do I think it resembles any other of his unusual compositions. The opening lines are: "This is Glenn speaking now. I had scarcely begun the first supper show of my gala season at the Maude Harbour festival when, as was my habit, I glanced toward the boxes, and there, seated on one marked 'Live bait. Do not refrigerate,' was a vision of such loveliness that it instantly erased from my mind the memory of all four amorous adventures that had befallen me between lunch and five o'clock."

This was jaw dropping. I thought it made Glenn sound like some Don Juan, a Casanova, until I understood it was a parody about two eminent pianists of the day: Arthur Rubinstein, known for boasting about his own celebrity and romantic conquests, and Rubinstein's former mentor and archrival, Vladimir Horowitz, whose return to the concert stage in 1965 after a twelve-year absence was widely publicized. Glenn delighted in poking this kind of mischievous fun at other concert pianists, although he too had retired from performing, but his producer took a different view and cut the section on Horowitz from the broadcast. Glenn revived the joke about Horowitz's prolonged sabbatical in his satirical 1980 Silver Jubilee Album, *A Glenn Gould Fantasy*. Of course, Maude Harbour never existed.

Glenn made me laugh. One time we ended up making all the farm animal noises we could think of, and he sang country and western songs he had composed. His voice was already distinctive, but his adding a twang to it made it unforgettable. He had written the songs as a teenager and was proud of these unlikely creations, even more self-satisfied than he usually was. He never did say what had inspired him.

Even though Glenn didn't have Hollywood movie star looks he was photographed a lot and had a great deal of charisma. Over time, he became an international music icon, which had decided drawbacks. His life became increasingly complicated. Publicity hounds, filmmakers, record producers, and besotted women tried to intervene in his carefully controlled life. Once he called Ray Roberts, his friend and manager, in the middle of the night to say a woman was pounding on his door. Then there was the woman from Texas who wrote to him every day. The music department secretary showed us her letters. This person said she was going to come to Canada and start shooting people unless he agreed to marry her. Of course, that just produced all the greater notoriety. Later, another woman insisted Glenn appeared to her several times in a train in the months after he died. We had no idea what to make of these sightings.

"Listen to the Music" had been on the air for several years by now and our audience was still growing. It took a lot of work to keep our classical music listeners engaged, and we heard from them all the time. A woman who worked in a university science department wrote, "Your program is excellent since it keeps me from falling asleep on the job (I count seeds). Thank you." I even heard from a woman who had been a student of my Hungarian aunt in the Sacred Heart Convent in Vienna in the 1950s. She sent a photo of Aunt Irene, which was a real surprise. We eventually discovered that Glenn was a regular listener, which pleased us no end. On one occasion, we featured a new recording of little-known early songs by Schoenberg. We announced a contest: free copies of the record to the first person who called in and identified the music. We waited and waited for the phone to ring but to our dismay, there was no response. Dead air. A broadcaster's nightmare. At last, the phone call light flashed on, Fredd answered, and it turned out to be Glenn. He said he could identify the piece, and he did. Fredd listened quietly then replied. "But Glenn, this is your latest recording we're giving away." Glenn responded: "I know, but I want my free record because I've identified it correctly." We mailed him out two copies the next day.

My mother, who was still teaching music and giving recitals in Princeton, alerted me to Glenn's second recording of the *Goldberg Variations* in 1981. She had begun to take notice of him in 1956 when his first recording of this Bach work was released and promoted on New York classical music stations. She bought the record and played it often. She was aware of the handsome young Canadian's eccentricities, dressing up for January weather in July, the piano chair with the sawed-off legs, his occasional odd tempos, and of course his humming along with his playing. It is audible on the *Goldberg Variations*, an idiosyncrasy she was prepared to overlook. My mother fervently believed that Glenn had a singular emotional, spiritual and musical connection with Bach.

I don't remember hearing Glenn's first Bach recording while I lived in Princeton, but I do remember seeing his photo on the cover. I was going on seventeen in 1956 and was sensitive to the charms of the handsome young stars of the day. He was no exception. The LP depicted a young man with matinee-idol good looks in a state of ecstasy. One was in black and white with "State of Wonder" written below the photograph, and the other, "The Birth of a Legend" in orange and brown. His unbuttoned shirt and ecstatic expression emphasized the physical effort of his playing. He certainly had the dark beauty and charisma to fascinate his public except for one detail. In person, he also had the self-effacing attitude of many Canadians, and he focused on one thing and one thing only, his music. When he finished recording the *Goldberg Variations* in the big Columbia studio, he quietly returned to Toronto. He did little if any socializing except with the technical recording team or the piano tuners. There was no barhopping, Stork Club, or Broadway shows for Glenn. He was twenty-three years old and would soon be dubbed the "Puritan."

On June 25, 1980, I was asleep when the phone rang at midnight. Startled, I thought it was a family emergency. But no, it was Glenn. He wanted to read me a script he had just finished. "It's not too late, is it?" "No, no, of course not," I said, sitting up in bed. So he began reading in his slightly pompous voice. Two hours later I had been introduced to "A Glenn Gould Fantasy." It was humorous but quirky, as so much of his written work was. Glenn knew I wasn't a musicologist, but he needed a "compare," his word. I had never been called one of those before, an announcer who serves as a moderator for a panel discussion. Glenn's idea was that we both played ourselves but also the other characters in the discussion. I would be two of them, the Hungarian character Márta Hortovány, the pied piper of the Kodály Kindergarten as well as Cassie Mackerel, a journalist with a strong southern drawl.

Glenn would play the parts of three of his favorite characters: Theodore Slutz, who had the looks and accent of a New York cab driver but who was supposedly, the fine arts editor of the *New York Village Grass is Greener*. His outfit, illustrated in the photo on the record cover, is hip – a white undershirt, black leather jacket and a flat cap. The pretentious English music critic Sir Nigel Twitt-Thornwaite had, like English comic actor Terry Thomas, more than a tinge of pomposity about him. As for Herr Karlheinz Klopweisser, renowned scholar and composer, Glenn later wrote in his record cover notes, "Klopweisser is currently at work on an analysis of Glenn Gould's 'Solitude Trilogy' which will be published in America under the title: 'Thematisch-systematisches Verzeichnis des Einsamkeit Trilogie von Glenn Gould.'" Always a good title. Glenn and I tried out our foreign accents on each other. His German and Russian were excellent. I couldn't mimic the Russian, and Glenn never managed the Hungarian lilt, which requires accenting the first syllable of each word. Theodore was my favorite character, and I urged Glenn to introduce him to Johnny Carson's late-night TV comedy audience. Naturally he declined.

That night, as he explained the idea to me, it never crossed my mind that it would end up as a CBS Masterworks recording, distributed all over the world, or that his loyal fans, including my parents, would be curious enough to buy it. What I did know was that working on this unusual project would be fun but challenging. Glenn was a perfectionist, and I worried that I would not be able to give him the support and tone he wanted. As it turned out we recorded this epic over two consecutive evenings at the Inn on the Park, a luxury hotel in a quiet setting in what was then a northeastern suburb of Toronto. Glenn kept a small ground-floor suite there, which he'd turned into a recording and editing studio. The receptionist at the front desk was instructed who and who not to let into the building.

I had heard that Glenn was a night owl, and his midnight phone call to me should have been enough to prove the rumour. But now I found out how true it was. He asked me to arrive at 9:00 p.m. to start work. We finished at 3:00 a.m. This was his usual work schedule, not mine. The technician, who arrived before me, had prepared all of Glenn's pre-recorded voices for the entire script. I followed the text, listening to the different characters saying their lines on my headphones, and Glenn, listening on his headphones, cued me for my response to them, which the technician recorded. Happily, we rehearsed first, and I became familiar with the different characters and laughed at their idiosyncrasies, which pleased Glenn. The work reminded me of the dubbing sessions I'd done years before in France. While Glenn was cuing me in with one hand, he was drumming on the tabletop with the other hand. I asked him what he was doing, and he said he was practising a Haydn sonata he planned to record soon. He said he always studied a piece that way before he ever played it on the piano.

Glenn had difficulty in settling down to work. At one point in our conversation, he referred to the 1967 "Idea of North," the first section of his *Solitude Trilogy*, the title of the record made of three documentaries he'd produced for the CBC. I reminded him I hadn't arrived in Canada until 1970. Without another word he wheeled his chair around, pulled a tape off the shelf and handed it to the technician. After listening to the woman's voice on the tape for the first twenty seconds or so, I burst into tears. It struck me as a eulogy to his loneliness. When the other voices joined this contrapuntal concerto, I found it deeply distressing. Glenn suffered so greatly physically from the cold and his self-inflicted isolation, and it occurred to me that with "Idea of North" and *Solitude Trilogy*, he was trying to control and confront his own fears.

Glenn reached over and took my hand in his. I knew about his fear of germs and distaste of physical contact. That just made me weep even more. But perhaps he was flattered by my reaction. My facile tears may have touched him. That was the only moment of spontaneous physical tenderness we ever had. After I stopped weeping, I excused myself and went to the adjoining bathroom to wipe away the tears. I was surprised to see pill bottles, large and small, covering the shelves and spilling over onto the sink. My mother had a similar collection, but her bottles were years out of date. Surely Glenn did the same thing, but I didn't examine his collection closely. When I emerged, more composed I said to Glenn, "My mother keeps all her medicine bottles forever but surely, you're not taking all of these?" "Well, no," he replied, "not all at once," and sort of laughed. That ended that conversation.

Mme Hortovány, my Hungarian character, was based on my mother – elegant, a strain of haughtiness, and slightly pedagogical, all carried off with a broad Hungarian accent. Fortunately, she never recognized herself in my loving parody. (Photo courtesy of CBC).

Before continuing our recording, we went through the closing section of "A Glenn Gould Fantasy." Glenn wanted my Hungarian character, Madame Hortovány, long preoccupied with the fascistic implications of the six-four chord in Richard Strauss, to speak about the prestigious Lenin Prize. I mentioned that no self-respecting Magyar would accept a Russian award and suggested a name such as the Pest Prize. Glenn considered this momentarily, but I saw a hint of annoyance pass over his face. He didn't like to be corrected, but he finally agreed to the more appropriate political statement. Madame Hortovány became the winner of the 1949 Pest Prize and was proud of it.

Glenn Gould's musical directions. Working on his fantasy Glenn said he knew exactly what he wanted, but that wasn't always clear to me. So Glenn's character, Dr. Karlheinz Klopweisser composed a musical score, "Margaret's Lied," to help me voice a phrase with the emphasis he wanted. It worked, too.

When we were well underway in the recording session, I ran into a line of text I didn't understand. I tried to say it with various intonations, but I couldn't find an interpretation that pleased us both. Glenn did not get impatient, but we did many takes and it still didn't make sense. When I arrived the next evening, he presented me with a page of sheet music. On it he had written several bars of melody in

Eb major (three flats or C minor) with the rhythm, and the text that I'd had difficulty with the night before. The score was dated July 1980 and signed in an elaborate script by Dr. Karlheinz Klopweisser, one of Glenn's characters – a convenient way for Glenn to remain at a distance. The lyrics read, "Margaret's Lied. Die Frage fur die Geschworenenliste. So, if one of you gentlemen would like to lead off with a question for Mr. Gould, then, oh well, perhaps we should have a little music first, just to get the interrogatory juices going and I can think of no more …etcetera." It was a very personal present, and Glenn knew I would keep it, and I have.

In the episode, Glenn expressed his own ideas in the German accent of Dr. Klopweisser and the pompous propositions of Sir Nigel. However, when Madame Hortovány asked Gould "whether it is not possible, like other artists who withdraw for a time from the public, then you make a hysterical return?" Glenn performed part of his long-delayed Horowitz sketch from Maude Harbor rejected seven years before by the CBC. Madame Hortovány's question regarding a hysterical return was the cue for the last section of the *Fantasy*, the glorious chaotic ending. It was a tumultuous offering provided by the sound effects man, a work of wild surrealism. It took twelve years for Vladimir Horowitz to return to Carnegie Hall in 1965, where he was greeted with astonishing approval. However, the two-disc Columbia recording of that concert had preserved every uncontrollable cough and clunker demonstrating Glenn's argument against live performances. The clarity achieved by editing a recording was far superior. Now at last, in the finale of the *Fantasy*, Glenn, who always yearned for total control, threw listeners into a world where the loss of control seems total by playing Ravel's *La Valse* at rocket speed. His version rose and fell with the crashing of waves of the Beaufort Sea in the background. It sounded as if Glenn's folding chair was washed overboard from his platform on the Geyser Exploratory Rig XB-67. The radio announcer said that Glenn was playing on his knees. But after the closing seconds of *La Valse*, came the sounds of Glenn walking off to the accompaniment of applause and the barks of a solitary seal. I don't know what Vladimir Horowitz thought of all of this. However, he was one of the first to send flowers upon hearing of Glenn's death.

A Glenn Gould Fantasy has its funny moments, but it was a cumbersome way to demonstrate his strong belief that recordings of recitals should not take place in uncontrolled environments.

After *Fantasy* came out, Glenn and I talked briefly about doing more projects together. He mentioned he'd written another satirical piece, *Nashville: Summer of 1914*, a take-off of Samuel Barber's *Knoxville Summer of 1915*, music I loved but he didn't really care for. It would be a parody of symphony committee ladies who lunch to raise money for concerts although they know little about music. I encouraged him, but it wasn't really his kind of takeoff. But for a chance encounter outside the Art Gallery of Ontario some months later, I never ran into him again. I heard he was working elsewhere on orchestral conducting projects and missed him, but realised it wasn't personal. He controlled his life by avoiding most close relationships. He used people and then dropped them because he had turned to someone and something else. Not because you had let him down, but his interests had simply changed. My work as his back-up person had strict limits. We never went out for a meal or coffee to gossip, except for one time at the Inn on the Park when we both drank fresh orange juice and Glenn ordered his usual scrambled eggs.

He did have one person he confided in, not just for a moment but over his lifetime. He and his cousin Jessie Grieg grew up together. She was the sister he never had, although she said that in their early years their conversation had been mostly banter. As time went by, it seemed to her that he lost the rigid self control he had always exercised. His mother's death in 1975 brought on a noticeable depression. His health concerns mounted, and he became consumed with thoughts of life after death and the spiritual plane.

Glenn died on October 4, 1982, days after his fiftieth birthday. He had had a stroke. Everyone was stunned. On October 15, one of those beautiful Toronto autumn days, a dozen or more of us from the CBC Radio music department walked over to the spacious St. Paul's Anglican Church on Bloor Street for his funeral. As we neared the church, we joined hundreds of people all heading in the same direction. We found seats midway up the large nave, but the church was soon standing room only. Afterward we learned over three thousand people attended. The Last Puritan, as he fancied himself, would have been pleased. All the major TV networks were represented, and TV cameras rolled up and down the aisles capturing our disconsolate expressions. The music was beautiful. Lois Marshall and Maureen Forester sang. Robert Aiken performed a flute concerto. When the service was over, the audience was emotionally drained and ready to leave. Then through the high rafters of the church, Glenn's voice came floating down, accompanying the "Aria," the opening thirty-two bars of Bach's *Goldberg Variations*. It was a climax of showmanship only Glenn could have created. No one moved. The cameras stopped rolling. It felt as if we had all ceased to breathe. We listened to him humming and singing along as he accompanied himself. The spell lasted long after the recording stopped. Everyone was silent or spoke in whispers as they made their way slowly out of the church, and as we walked back to our little world of music in the CBC Radio building none of us said a word.

François Girard's fine 1993 film *Thirty-Two Short Films about Glenn Gould* includes interviews with many of us who knew Glenn, with actor Colm Feore playing Glenn. In it, Jessie Grieg speaks about Glenn's desire to attend his own funeral to see how many people show up. Glenn had told her he was convinced nobody would come. Jessie pointed out that people all over the world were buying his records. When she saw the crowd pouring into his funeral "I thought he was wrong for perhaps the first time in his life. He was never wrong." He was proved wrong.

Glenn was buried in the Gould family plot in Mount Pleasant

Cemetery, the oldest burial ground in the city. In the fall of 1999, John Miller, a noted cultural administrator and the Executive Director of the Glenn Gould Foundation organized a gathering of Glenn's friends and collaborators for a grave-side service of remembrance. It took place on a beautiful day when the air was clear, the red and gold leaves rustled gently, providing a colorful backdrop to our reunion. Chairs were placed around and in front of the grave site and the speaker's podium. John had asked me to introduce the service. I told him I might not be able to do this as the tears were about to flow. But I still tried. After my noticeably brief introduction, he carried on. The event was a success. Family and close friends reminisced about Glenn, and by the end we all felt more at peace, surrounded by the quiet cemetery, having had a chance to express our loss. Glenn would have enjoyed our modestly embroidered recollections of his musical voyage.

He would have also enjoyed Girard's film, which he co-wrote with Don McKellar. It has done a service for all of us who worked with Glenn. Many organizations subsequently interviewed us: the BBC, NHK-Japanese television, authors, representatives from CBS Records, Sony and others. Girard's film kept us honest. We could have enhanced our relationships with Glenn, but I believe we all have had the curious notion that, whenever someone turned on the mic, Glenn was sitting in the chair opposite, head in hand, listening intently, obliging us to be honest and straightforward about him.

Glenn is recognized as one of the most acclaimed musicians of the twentieth century. In 1977 the United States government launched two Voyager spacecrafts destined to pass Jupiter and Saturn in their journey to the edge of the solar system and perhaps beyond. Glenn's performance of the prelude and fugue in C major from the first book of Bach's *Well-Tempered Clavier* is one of the pieces of music and other sounds from Earth aboard. The Voyagers are now somewhere out beyond the planets, and everything is on schedule.

Chapter 13

Picnic basket surprise

When we got married, Bob and I were already thinking of having children. As a teenager, I had lots of experience looking after youngsters. They were never a problem; it was the parents who occasionally caused trouble. But I had no experience with newborns, and Bob admitted he wasn't very interested in them. We were both frightened by their helplessness and fragility and the possible consequences of our almost total ignorance. All we knew for sure was that it is a good idea to support the baby's head for their first few months. Our ignorance probably put us in the same boat as a lot of other prospective parents, but there was little comfort in the thought. We weren't daunted, though.

Bob knew about my pregnancy scare in Paris back in the 1960s. But this was unlike the past. Here I was, twenty years later in a different relationship with a man I love and have married. I dearly wanted to have his child. When I arrived in Canada in 1970, a doctor advised me to use an IUD rather than the birth control pill. So I did until the day I was at a gym class, jumping and flailing about with the others and had the uncomfortable realization the device had fallen out. As the years went by, I felt an increasing urgency to have a baby. Bob has a large family of aunts, uncles, and cousins. We were just the four of us in Princeton. There were many relatives, but they were all in Hungary, and no one came to visit even after the Second World

War. My sister has two daughters, my nieces. They are delightful young women and have visited us in Toronto several times. But they and their parents all live in Alaska.

I was now in my early forties, and we still had no babies, but not for want of trying. I had one miscarriage after another, and my gynecologist enrolled me in an experimental program to help older women to conceive and carry their babies to term. We tried everything, mostly rest. Once when I was twelve weeks pregnant, after several days of quiet, I spied a mouse running across the floor in our bedroom. I jumped out of bed and ended up in the Wellesley Hospital for yet another D&C (dilation and curettage). My doctor gave me hormones to keep their levels balanced, but depression set in, and I couldn't go to work. I was frightened CBC would replace me on "Listen to the Music." Fredd said that wouldn't happen because the audience was used to my voice, and they hate change. Staying on the job mattered to me, especially staying at CBC, where unexpected opportunities for women often came up.

My doctor, who was also my friend, gave me a book to read to encourage me to stay in bed. It was a 1000-page diverse collection by Voltaire, a somewhat heavy volume to rest on my stomach. I did manage to read all of it, although through no fault of Voltaire's I ended up in hospital once again. This time a Christmas choir was singing in the lobby, the conductor was Robert Cooper, a colleague from CBC. I was sitting in a wheelchair in the audience, regretting that I was not the radio announcer for his holiday concert, and feeling sorry for myself. Not exactly a Christmas spirit.

Bob, the doctor, and I were beginning to think this baby is never meant to be. We were all concerned about my mood swings and overall health. I couldn't keep spending weeks resting in bed or in the hospital or keep scheduling lovemaking. It was easy to discuss all these issues with my doctor, but I had no women friends to talk to about being old and attempting to have a baby. None of them had had that experience themselves. Bob and I decided to try one last time. Once again, I conceived, and six weeks later the doctor did an ultrasound. Bob stayed with me for the procedure, as he always did. Sadly, the fetus showed no life but suddenly we began to hear a voice, it was indistinct but seemed to be coming from somewhere deep inside me. We looked at each other, then back at the ultrasound image. It was a voice all right and as we bent in to listen more closely, we began to make out words. "Forty-two, you're first. Sixteen … Twenty-two for four Ave and Bloor …" It was a dispatcher at a taxi company radioing its drivers. The doctor had never heard any voices emanating from his ultrasound machine. We all laughed, which lightened the mood for a moment. In the end, we agreed to abandon our attempts to have a baby. It would be sad not to have a child with Bob's beautiful brown hair and my blue eyes, but the hardest part for me was accepting I was too old.

Instead, in 1981, we started to think about adoption. I had the good fortune to provide voiceovers throughout the years for David Suzuki's still on the air award-winning series the "Nature of Things." I was such a fan, I would have paid him to participate in his fascinating documentaries. The programs were always compelling, especially one about saving the endangered whooping crane from extinction and the development in India of the artificial foot. Another I worked on that had special meaning for us, "Black-Market Babies," was about how well-off Canadians brought young, blond, and pregnant Irish girls to Canada to have their babies and be handsomely rewarded for their efforts. The cost to the adoptive parents was ten thousand dollars or more.

We didn't try to find out if this black-market activity still existed, but we did go to Children's Aid and were invited to an evening film presentation of children available for adoption. With some uneasiness, we joined a dozen other prospective parents to see projected images of children of ages up to fourteen while an administrator described their background, health, and history. At the end of the presentation, we were invited to speak with one of the administrators about the child or children we were interested in. The person we spoke with was blunt, to say the least. It was a painful and unpleasant interview. We asked about adopting a newborn or, at least, a younger child than we had been shown. She told us we were too old, too highly educated, too wealthy and would have lofty expectations of the child, suggesting they would be unlikely to be met by any of their children. Still, she said, there were two children from a First Nations family, seven and eight years old, who had been in foster care for years, we might qualify to adopt them. Their three siblings would be placed in another home.

We learned later that most of the children presented that evening had behavioral problems or daunting medical issues. A few acquaintances who had adopted older children had shared their experiences with us, and all had said their children had great difficulty adjusting to their family. With feelings of regret and guilt we told Children's Aid we didn't feel qualified to take on such a responsibility. We walked away, saddened by the stories of these children, and discouraged to realize we didn't have the psychological skills or the determination to raise children with such complex needs.

But after considerable research, we discovered a small private agency – just two people, a lawyer, and a former employee of one of the large provincial adoption agencies. They agreed to help us find a newborn baby here in Canada. Their age limit for parents was forty-three, so I just passed the requirements. There would be twelve hours of interviews, we would need two letters of reference, and the cost would be $1100.

We got to know the social worker well and she us, which was the purpose of these visits, of course. She came to our house three time, saw the room we had set aside as baby's room, looked at the back yard, visited the local children's playgrounds, and discussed our ideas on how to bring up a child. We asked her where the agency found newborns, and she explained that nurses in hospital maternity wards usually knew which of their patients did not want to keep their babies. She was in contact with many of them and considered it the most reliable way to find healthy babies. She said she thought our old downtown house was, well, interesting but discreetly did not say, as we had come to realize, it was not ideal for young children. It was drafty, even cold to some tastes, had splintery wooden floors and just about every flat surface was home to books, papers, photographs, models, trinkets, and mementos from years of travel.

As part of the interview process, we visited her in her home. It was a split-level suburban house, fully carpeted, painted entirely white and without a toy, shoe or even cushion out of place. Every flat surface we could see was clear and empty. Well almost empty. Empty except for the collection of owls that Bob uncharitably said as we left looked like prizes from the CNE. They weren't, but they were everywhere: plaster owls, large and small, all of them brown with flat faces and big yellow eyes. He was sure they were carefully arranged to stare directly at us. Bob never has felt comfortable with psychologists and social workers, and those creepy owls did nothing to ease his anxiety here.

Assuming the owls were an elaborate psychological test, we pretended not to notice them. We must have passed it and the other tests because our social worker (who was really very nice) and the lawyer with whom she worked agreed to do all they could to find us a baby. But they cautioned, don't expect to know anything about the child, their mother or father or their background, nor even what hospital they were born in. The answer to our incredulous questions was always "That's just the way it is."

Now there was nothing to do but wait. I knew nothing about newborns and had no maternity classes to help me learn what to do in the baby's early months. I was impatient, but the doctor reminded me that babies are a gift, you cannot demand one to appear. But during the summer of 1982, I did get help for my chronic mood swings, and almost a month after Glenn died, on October 29 at eight o'clock in the morning, our social worker called to say that she had a healthy baby boy of a racially mixed background. Did we still want to go ahead with the adoption? I said I'd talk to Bob and call her right back. We had fifteen minutes to decide, she said. I sat on the front hall steps, Bob paced around the hall. Our big concern was how the child would come to feel about having white parents. But there was only one way to find out. We decided to say yes, of course we would.

Our lives abruptly changed. We had to do everything parents usually have months to prepare for but do it all immediately. Bob's family stepped in, and we soon found ourselves with a crib, blankets, diapers, bottles, sterilizers, formula, and beautiful baby clothes. Someone contributed a well-thumbed Dr. Spock's book on baby care, which I sorely needed and someone else donated a baby carriage and a baby sling. We were given things we didn't know we would need. It was overwhelming. Six days later, on November 4, two lawyers knocked on the door carrying a picnic basket with our baby nestled inside. They placed the basket on the kitchen table, shook hands with both of us, wished us good luck and walked out. We stood there looking down at the baby boy sleeping peacefully in the basket, totally dumbfounded and uncertain what to do. Should we pick him up, let him sleep, feed him, change him? We couldn't decide, so we just stood there and watched him for a while. With the sudden and growing realization of the momentousness of our situation, we called Bob's mother for advice.

She soon arrived to help. But there was panic the first few days as I thought he had convulsions. Much to my relief, Dr. Spock's book assured me that it was only hiccups. We surely needed help, though. And we found it through friends in the form of a wonderful woman from the Victorian Order of Nurses, who like Mary Poppins arrived on the west wind, incredibly enough, in a starched white uniform and nurse's cap. She knew all about babies, hiccups and the rest and taught me a lot. She also listened to the CBC, an added benefit since she wanted me to go back to "Listen to the Music" as soon as possible.

One of the first things we had to decide was what to name him. I wanted to call him Glenn, but with Campbell as his family name, there was a risk he would be associated with country singer Glen Campbell, the "Wichita Lineman". So he became Andrew, a Scottish name that has nothing to do with telephone poles and a wistful lineman.

In 1982, CBC offered only two weeks maternity benefit for an adoption. After this period was over it meant I would have to give up work and stay home to look after the baby. I couldn't do that. We hadn't really thought about how the baby's arrival would impact my career. I had a modest following at CBC and loved most of the programs that came my way.

Baby Andrew at three months' old. Andrew smiled a lot, in fact so often that it seemed as if we had met before.

Our Mary Poppins looked after Andrew during the daytime for the first month after I went back to work, but she finished at about the time I got home. So I had the night shift. It was tiring, but that's how I discovered an all-night jazz station broadcasting out of Chicago and gave our son his 4:00 a.m. bottle to the sounds of Coltrane and Charlie Parker.

She was wonderful, but she specialized in newborn babies, and I knew she couldn't stay with us long. One of my colleagues at work put us in touch with an agency for nannies run by her mother. A young Swiss woman named Sonja came for an interview and ended up staying with us for two and a half years. By the time she arrived, Andrew was sleeping through the night and so was I. It was a relief to get uninterrupted sleep at last, but I missed listening to the jazz broadcast in the wee small hours from Chicago.

Chapter 14

Meeting the ravens

The first year of working full-time at CBC and being a mum was difficult but manageable because we had a lot of help, and Andrew was a happy, playful baby. "Listen to the Music" was in its tenth year of being on the air at the same time and from the same studio. Our neighbors in the studio next door, the "Royal Canadian Air Farce", had been on CBC Radio just as long. The Farceurs changed over the years, but in 1984 they were Don Ferguson, Roger Abbott, Luba Goy, and Dave Broadfoot. We ran into each other in the hallway all the time, and they often entertained me with an off-the-cuff analysis of the current political situation that left me in stitches. They knew I was a loyal fan.

One day Roger Abbott stopped me in the hallway to tell me the Farce had been invited to the inauguration of a cultural centre in Yellowknife, Northwest Territories. It would be a gala evening on May 21. Unfortunately, Luba Goy was unable to go. Would I be interested in standing in for her? I thought he was joking. Luba never missed a program. But he was serious. Could I join the "Royal Canadian Air Farce" and fly to the far north of Canada? I jumped at the chance of working with them and told him I probably could find time to do this. Roger explained they would record two separate episodes in front of a live audience, and there would be a complete run-through of the scripts before the show. I accepted the offer with pleasure after consulting Bob and Sonja, our Swiss nanny. Bob immediately clued in that I wanted to go with the Farceurs, and they assured me they could look after Andrew for four days.

We were a group of eight, including the two dependable script writers, a production assistant, and Maritimer Johnny Dalton, who for years had produced this chaotic masterpiece with patience and focus. We flew first to Winnipeg, where we changed planes for a noisy older four-motor aircraft. I knew nothing about Yellowknife, except that it was the capital of the Northwest Territories, and the trip north seemed endless. We finally arrived at dusk. The land was rock ground down by an ancient ice age. There were no trees to speak of, and the vast Great Slave Lake stretched out of sight. The town, a collection of wooden buildings dotted among rocky knolls, was located on the shore of an immense bay.

The organizers of the gala event settled us in the four-storey hotel, the tallest building in town at that time. The next morning, as I stepped out of the hotel for a walk I heard loud cawing. There were ravens perched everywhere: on bushes, buildings, and telephone lines. I learned later that, in Dene culture, ravens calling during the daytime was a good omen, but calling at night meant bad fortune. I walked to the edge of town and came to an unusual sight. Situated next to the tall Welcome to Yellowknife sign was an exceptionally large airplane, a Bristol Freighter, sitting atop a concrete pedestal, with "Wardair," painted in large letters on its side. Legendary bush pilot Max Ward started a freight service out of Yellowknife in the mid 1940s. Wardair eventually became a national charter airline, carrying thousands of passengers around the world.

Continuing my walk, I came upon some large green cylinders, about five feet in diameter, made of corrugated metal culvert pipe. Each had a heavy metal screen sealing one end, and the other end had a guillotine-like door. I asked a passerby what they were. Bear traps, he said. The town had a bear problem, and it wasn't just seasonal. When they became a nuisance, city workers trapped and relocated them.

The ravens weren't the only creatures making a commotion that morning. As I walked around the more residential district, raucous yelps and growls greeted me. High fences around well-maintained properties enclosed teams of sled dogs, all apparently eager to set off for a run. They were far from friendly, so I turned back to the midtown shopping area, which was busy with shoppers on foot and the traffic of battered pick-up trucks. I entered a tourist shop to look at Inuit soapstone carvings, a voice was blaring that I recognized. It was Peter Gzowski, host of "Morningside," CBC Radio's popular daily morning program. Was there any place in Canada where his familiar voice didn't reach? Probably not, but it was sort of comforting to hear a well-known voice while approximately five thousand kilometres from home.

Hanging out in Yellowknife with the "Air Farce" members the day before our show. From the left, CBC Radio producer John Dalton, Roger Abbot, me and Don Ferguson. Missing here was Dave Broadfoot. (Photo courtesy of CBC).

We rehearsed the final scripts before the evening's performance.

They seemed funny but not uproariously so. Roger explained something I had never seriously encountered before. The audience could laugh at unexpected moments, and we had to be prepared to pause. If they didn't laugh when we expected, then he or Don might make an ad lib remark about their silence. Just be prepared. In any case, all three of them would be there to back me up, and they wouldn't leave me with dead air, a broadcaster's nightmare. The programs were being taped for later broadcast, which meant we didn't have to begin exactly at 8:00 p.m. and end at 8:59. If something didn't work, we could rerecord the section. Apparently, live audiences didn't mind these kinds of mistakes. This took a lot of the pressure off.

It was an elegant event. A make-up artist worked her magic, and I wore a long shimmery green dress. The auditorium was newly decorated, and at least three hundred people applauded enthusiastically when we walked on stage. Although I was short of breath at the beginning, I managed to get through the script without too many mishaps. I laughed at Don and Roger's ad libs a bit too often and Don cracked a joke whenever I flubbed a line, which made my errors seem part of the script. The audience thought we had planned all the hi-jinks.

After our performance, we were invited to a reception at the theatre manager's home. We were offered generous amounts to drink and delicacies including Arctic char, a northern fish that tasted much like smoked salmon. There was music and I discovered to my delight that Dave Broadfoot was a splendid ballroom dancer. He invited me to tango, and I tried my best, but he was very tall, which made him hard to follow. Roger had a quieter manner on the dance floor. At two in the morning the sun was still just above the horizon. We watched the shimmering colours of the northern lights – waving green and yellow curtains suspended in the atmosphere and reflected in the waters of Great Slave Lake. It seemed as if we were floating out to sea on a magical Viking raft. It was mesmerizing.

Roger and I sat together on the long return flight to Toronto.

Neither of us had much to say because the farther south we flew, the more this unusual excursion seemed like a dream. I did tell him how proud I was to be part of the "Air Farce," even if it were for only this one time. CBC network radio broadcast the programs coast to coast, and we all did sound funny.

    Unfortunately for me anyway, Luba Goy never missed another program in her many years as a member of this brilliant, endearing group of entertainers. Back home I received hugs from Andrew, and everybody was glad to see me. Did I have a good trip? Yes, but all I could say was it felt like a voyage to another world.

Chapter 15

The Pope and the baby

That year, 1984, was special in many ways. Not only did I go to Yellowknife, but I got to hang out with the Pope. Well, not quite. But Pope John Paul II made the first of his two visits to Toronto that year. Some three hundred thousand of his devoted followers turned out for a special mass on September 15 at the former Downsview airbase. I wasn't there, but the day before the mass I attended the ecumenical service to greet his Eminence held at St. Paul's Cathedral, where two years earlier so many of us had gathered for Glenn Gould's funeral. It turned out to be an extraordinary gathering.

I'm not a Catholic. I'm not even a church goer, but someone in the Catholic Church in Toronto thought it would be appropriate for me to read a Biblical text at the service. The request was sent to one of the CBC's vice-presidents and passed on to me through the announce office. It was a breathtaking invitation and despite my decided lack of churchly qualifications, one I could not turn down. It was a Saturday anyway, so it wouldn't take me away from my regular program work. I enjoyed stopping by my boss's desk to tell him that if anything came up that Saturday not to schedule me because, well, I'd be with the Pope.

I received a copy of the passage several days before the service. A German woman was to read a passage in French after I had delivered one in English. There was no rehearsal and surprisingly little security. I was just given a time and told to make my way to the front of the church.

Before the service began, the bishops from many different sects – Armenians, Greek Orthodox, Church of Antioch, Russian Orthodox – all welcomed me warmly. They were an elegant-looking group, with dark flowing beards, and luxurious white robes variously trimmed in purple and gold and red. Bishop Sotirios of the Greek Diocese gave the opening prayer. Singers from St. Paul's choir and the St. Michael's Choir School sang together and separately, filling the vaulted roof with choruses of "Jubilate Deo," "Gloria Deo," "Exultate Justi" and a doxology from the Christian church popular in about 1100 AD. Then Pope John Paul II entered and offered a greeting. He stood quietly in front of the altar for a few moments of meditation, then he and the congregation sat down, and our two readings followed. My brief passage was the first, and I had to deliver it from the pulpit high above the nave. To reach it meant climbing up several narrow and dangerous looking stairs. I arrived at the top very nervous and feeling slightly dizzy. Dear God, I was thinking, don't let me faint now. I reached for the edge of the lectern. The service was being broadcast live by all three national television networks. It was another one of those terrifying public appearances, like reading the television bulletin about the fall of Saigon. I always say yes to these things but end up being so frightened I can scarcely move. Why did I agree to do them when they caused so much distress? Was it the challenge? I don't know the answer. I didn't have much time to think about it before some church official discretely pointed to me. It was my turn to read. Isaiah 58, verses six through eleven. My voice echoed through the church. All was quiet when I concluded the passage. I descended slowly and carefully, then passed immediately in front of His Eminence. He looked at me and smiled and I at him. Maybe it was just light-headedness, but I felt very warm and happy.

In June, Charlotte, my best friend from Miss Fine's School days whose family had a house in Martha's Vineyard invited us to stay with her for a week. Andrew, now two and a half years old, was old enough to make the trip. The flight from Toronto to Boston was uneventful. Andrew was interested in the passengers, looked out the window at the clouds and charmed a flight attendant, who fed him a steady stream of snacks. In Boston's Logan airport, while we waited for a vintage DC-3 to shuttle us to the Vineyard, Andrew ran in circles around the small waiting room. After a few circuits, like a boomerang, he dashed back to his stroller, fortunately before the other, scowling passengers felt compelled to offer us their views on child rearing. We boarded the old airplane and after a short low-level flight we landed in Edgartown. The highlights of the trip for me were the fun times Andrew had. He spent hours playing on the beach. The waves were gentle, and he dug holes in the sand and watched them rapidly fill with water. In Oak Bluffs, one of the older villages on the Vineyard, there was, and still is, a colourful antique merry-go-round. The Flying Horses Carousel is the oldest operating platform carousel still running in the United States. Built in New York in 1876 it has two sets of twenty horses placed side by side, all beautifully decorated in a rainbow of colours. The horseback riders try to grab a ring as they ride by, the prize for getting it being a free ride. The music sounds like accordions and organs playing parade pieces from the 1930s. Bob and Andrew took several turns on one horse, with Andrew holding on to the pole in front, but didn't manage to catch a brass ring. It was a happy trip all around.

Just as we arrived home and walked into the front hall, we heard the telephone ringing. Andrew ran off happy to see Sonja, and Bob picked up the receiver. It was the social worker who had played such an important part in Andrew's adoption. Bob and I stood stock still, looking at each other as he held the receiver so we could both hear her. We knew why she was calling. She had asked some months after Andrew arrived if we were interested in adopting another child later

"Well, yes," we had said tentatively, more out of politeness than conviction and too sleep deprived to think straight. Now she told us a baby was due a few days later around the first of July. Were we interested? We said we would call back shortly.

We had a lot to think about. Could we do this again? First, there was my age, now forty-seven, and our challenging jobs to consider. We called my mother in Princeton, spoke to Bob's mother and to Charlotte whom we had just left in Martha's Vineyard and who was keenly aware of the time and effort we devoted to Andrew. They all listened carefully and advised us against a second adoption. So, of course, we decided to welcome another child.

Our second Swiss nanny, also named Sonja, was herself adopted. She thought it was a wonderful idea, even though it would be more work for her too. We called the social worker and said yes, we would be thrilled. Then the countdown began. July 1 came and went without a word from anyone, as did every day of the following week. By then we were worried. On July 10, thirty seconds before "Listen to the Music" went to air, the social worker called me at work. Fredd answered the phone and told her to hold for a few minutes. The red cue light flashed on, and I said, "Good evening. Welcome to Listen to the Music." As soon as I had introduced the first piece of music, Fredd put in the call. The social worker gave me the news that our healthy baby girl had arrived the night before weighing eight pounds. I have no recollection of how we got through those first minutes of the program, but I reached Bob, who moments earlier in a studio on the other side of the old radio building had just cued Elizabeth Gray and Al Maitland to start "As It Happens." He was delighted it was a little girl and said he would call the social worker as soon as they had cued a taped interview. Meanwhile Fredd and my technician broke out the champagne they'd scrounged from somewhere and we raised our glasses to my new baby daughter. What an unusual situation for two expectant parents. Both of us on air coast to coast at the same time and getting news about a new daughter, truly a wonderful gift. Once again performance triumphs.

It took us a while to settle in with Alexandra Charlotte, named after two of my close friends. She had colic for the first few weeks. Every afternoon at six she would start crying, a dreaded moment not just for me, but for everyone in the house and our neighbours. It wasn't just six o'clock, of course, and it was relentless. There seemed to be little we could do to comfort her. That was the frightening part. The real problem, though, was that Alexandra had an exceptionally loud voice, and the energy to use it for a long time. The summer nights were warm, so we walked around and around outside the house, often at two o'clock in the morning trying to console her, hoping in vain not to wake up the neighbors. When Alexandra cried, people walking on the street could hear her. It was like carrying a car alarm.

Baby Alexandra at 7 months old, a lovely and happy baby.

It was an ordeal for all of us. Not much you can do, our pediatrician said, adding children with colic are often unusually smart and full of energy. Maybe, but that rosy promise was of little comfort at that moment. I was sleepless, anguished and frustrated and it was then my sister Anne arrived from Alaska. I'd told her about Alexandra's strident bouts of colic, but she brushed it off and came anyway. Maybe she could sleep in a tent in the backyard, I thought, or stay in a hotel or stay home even. We were all prepared for the harrowing nightly anguish, but as six neared and we nervously watched the clock, she picked the baby up. Alexandra smiled, we waited, nothing happened. Alexandra went back to sleep. My sister, the mother of two, said she couldn't see anything unusual about this child. Alexandra never had another colic attack, peace descended on our household, and my sister took all the credit.

Chapter 16

No love for torch singers at "The Kremlin"

Once Alexandra was over the early colicky months, I thought about using my own voice and picking up my singing where I had left off years earlier. During my time in France, I had taken lessons with Mme Queru, a voice teacher who instructed me in the early twentieth-century lyrical repertoire of French composers, including Debussy, Fauré, and Poulenc. Somehow through her contacts I was invited one afternoon to meet the celebrated French classical music teacher and conductor Nadia Boulanger, who once coached Fauré, Aaron Copland, Astor Piazzolla, and even jazz man Quincy Jones – everyone except George Gershwin. The story goes that in 1927, the twenty-nine-year-old Gershwin, who was living in Paris at the time, visited her. She knew of his work –*Rhapsody in Blue*, the extraordinary fusion of jazz and classical music had debuted in New York three years earlier. They talked over tea for half an hour in her rooms. Finally, Gershwin asked if she would teach him composition. Mlle Boulanger is said to have looked at him for a moment then saying, "M. Gershwin, I can teach you nothing." The next year he composed *An American in Paris*.

When I was an American in Paris, Mlle Boulanger's reputation in the musical world was still formidable, but she was just as well known for the tea parties she gave regularly to introduce her students to one another. When I contacted her about singing lessons, she invited me to the next gathering at her apartment just a block south of the Moulin Rouge and the Carrousel de Paris. I walked by these gaudy tourist traps on my way to my first tea party, feeling nervous about meeting her. In the photos I'd seen, she looked stern, but she greeted me with great warmth and introduced me to the young American piano student among her guests that day. Her famous grand piano was covered with photos of many of her well-known pupils. After a while she served tea, neglecting to mention that she had poured a liberal amount of rum into the teapot. The party soon became livelier, and she continued to pour us more tea. Eventually, we all felt like old friends. I don't remember a great deal of what we talked about, only that we spoke in many languages – Italian, Portuguese, Greek and American English. It was a lovely, gray November afternoon, and it had left me feeling that we had been in an impressionist painting of handsome young men in straw hats and young women in long, ruffled dresses reclining under a pastoral shaded glen.

Now, in Toronto, I asked around and found a teacher at the Royal Conservatory of Music who agreed to help me recover my vocal range after so many years without practice. I wanted to sing the music that appealed to me –not Debussy and Poulenc but the classics of the Great American Songbook by George Gershwin, Cole Porter, and others up to about 1960. Many of its songs were performed by the great female vocalists of the late thirties and forties – Edith Piaf, Judy Garland, Ella Fitzgerald, Billie Holiday – and the torch singers, now largely forgotten. They were the ones I'd fallen in love with and wanted to rediscover.

I focused on six of them. Helen Morgan was the first and probably the quintessential torch singer. She was born in 1900 on the other side of the tracks in small-town Ohio. But could she sing. Her plaintive laments for lost love made her a hit in Chicago clubs in the twenties. She could dance too and made it into the big-time dancing in the Ziegfeld Follies. When Jerome Kern discovered her, he cast her in the leading role in one of the first musicals *Showboat*. She died of alcoholism at forty-one. She fit into my list of torch singers nicely.

Next came Ethel Waters or Sweet Mama Stringbean, born in 1896 to a penniless twelve-year-old girl in Chester, Pennsylvania. She became one of the first Black singers to have a go at "white time," making it from Harlem to Hollywood. Religion was her addiction. Another was Libby Holman, who came from a once-wealthy family in Cincinnati and paid her way through university as a sex worker. She was brash, independent, an acclaimed actress and a phenomenal singer, but only when she felt like it. Her marriages were disastrous, but her second husband left her $4 million. She died at sixty-seven of carbon monoxide poisoning, depressed, sitting in her white Rolls Royce.

Billie Holiday was yet another child of the slums. Her mother was thirteen when Billie was born. Early on she sang in speakeasies in Harlem and, like Ethel Waters, had a go at "white time," travelling with Artie Shaw's band as late as 1938. But it was a whites-only world then, and she was shut out of it. She died a heroin addict at the age of forty-four. We know more about Billie's life than the other blues singers of this generation thanks to her unique voice and style. The pain of her story comes through in the way she shapes her songs. It's hard to listen to her cry for help, but she remains my favorite of the group.

Alice Faye, born in 1915, had a lovely alto voice, as well as blonde curls and blue eyes, and as a teenager landed a role in a Broadway musical. Rudy Vallée heard her sing, and she joined his society orchestra. She went on to make thirty-two movies in eleven years, married band leader Phil Harris, and made time to raise two children. She was approachable, unpretentious and had a relatively untroubled life. The sixth of my choices was big band singer Jane Froman. She had an extensive following in the forties, entertaining American soldiers abroad. But in 1943, her plane crashed in Portugal, leaving her unable to walk except on crutches. Two years later, she resumed singing for the troops in Europe. A film was later made of her life, *With a Song in My Heart*. It starred Susan Hayward but Jane Froman sang all the songs.

   Nowadays few people have heard of these vocalists. Torch singers have an intimate, vulnerable style, suited for small venues, not the huge stadiums where today's popular singers perform. In the 1950s I saw many movies where women played glamorous night club singers performing the vocals themselves or having the singing dubbed for them. I dreamed of telling their personal stories, singing some of their hits and capturing their allure.

   At the time I was researching these bygone artists, the mood swings which had affected me for years started to occur more frequently and with greater intensity. It was 1985, and I was nearing fifty, and my doctor said it likely was just menopause. I didn't want to argue with her as she had always offered me sage advice over the years, but I told her I'd been experiencing moments of depression or elation since my early twenties. And they were getting worse and harder to pass off as excitement or just a bad day at the office. Now it was beginning to affect my family. I was often moody for days on end, losing my temper for no reason, then becoming depressed by my own behaviour. The children and Bob don't know which version of me would show up at any given day or hour or what they had done to make me so angry. I didn't know either.

   A friend who knew how bad these mood swings had become lent me her apartment on the fifteenth floor of a nearby high-rise to use when I needed to get away. I would feed the children supper then retire to this lofty retreat. I don't remember what I did there, only that I spent a lot of time on the balcony looking over the treetops and listening to my old jazz records. At dusk I would slide into a very dark place, then struggle my way unsteadily to dawn, only to coast through the day and back into darkness. I began to drink a lot of gin, followed by rum to fall asleep. I was fearful and anxious, knowing what I felt, but unable to control it, which in turn made me angry and depressed. There were frightening moments, when I leant over the balcony railing feeling sick and dizzy from fighting the urge to jump. I became so alarmed that I could do myself real harm that I went back to my doctor. I told her everything that had occurred during the past few weeks, explaining I felt like I was riding a Ferris wheel up to the top, holding my breath for five seconds, then plunging down again. I no longer had any control over my life. I told her I feared losing everything, the man I love and the two children we adored. The doctor didn't have any specific solution but suggested we meet at least once a week to talk about how I manage to cope with my home life, my work at CBC and my research on my torch singers. She became part of my life and helped me get through many difficult years.

    I kept working on the musical project, but the mood swings were probably not helped by learning more about the sad lives of these singers. The whole venture was emotionally heavy. I was careful about the music I chose though. I tried to find a middle ground between their most heartrending laments and cheerful "Tea for Two" ditties. During all my research, I discovered "Strange Fruit," a powerful song protesting the lynchings of Blacks in the American South recorded by Billie Holiday in 1939. It became the most important political song of its time and is said to be the beginning of the civil rights movement in the United States. It was not really a song for me. Mine is a cheery, mezzo-soprano voice not made for intense passion or heartbreak, but I can get a good story across in key.

    I did all my research in the cramped music library in the cellar of the old CBC Radio building which had the reference books, records, and newspaper clippings I needed. I asked the librarians for information about my torch singers, and they went to work enthusiastically, glad of the change from the usual requests for politically apt songs. Suddenly I had stacks of material about the little-known Libby Holman and Alice Faye. They found newspaper stories detailing the chaotic lifestyles of Billie Holiday and Ethel Waters and the painful racism of the time. Putting my script together was still hard work, and Bob helped, but without the diligent CBC librarians, I couldn't have done it at all. I gave my final draft to a professional writer, Amanda McConnell, from the "Nature of Things," to check over. It is complete except for a title. Friends assured me that coming up with the right title is often the most difficult part. That winter, Bob and I spent a week in the Caribbean where I tried to memorize my script. Every afternoon we sat by the sea and went over and over the text and the words of the songs, but I had great difficulty in remembering any of them. My mood swings were damaging my ability to retain the exact wording.

Back in Toronto, a guitar player friend Willy Wilson knocked at our door one day with a gold-framed picture tucked under his arm. "Surprise!" he said. It was the front cover of sheet-music, bearing the movie title *Gold Diggers of 1933* in a yellow slash. Below the slash is a glamorous photo of Ginger Rogers and above it is the title of one of the hit numbers, "I've Got to Sing a Torch Song," by the songwriters Al Dubin and Harry Warren. I had found my title. It was perfect.

The CBC librarians unearthed an early recording of the movie so I could hear the slightly muffled soundtrack. It helped me better understand the vocal style of the time. Norm Abbott, my teacher at the Conservatory of Music, who had already agreed to be my piano accompanist, also thought the title was exactly right. Together, we selected the songs that best represented each of the six singers, and then I had to make sure that I could sing them. It took a while but finally we had a script, the music, a title – all the makings of a one-hour show. All we needed was a theatre. Friends encouraged me to approach the artistic director of the Studio Theatre, a small playhouse on the third floor above the Young People's Theatre. The YPT's artistic director was enthusiastic. We shook hands and agreed on the dates. *I've Got to Sing a Torch Song* would run for six nights at 8:00 p.m., from Monday, March 3, 1986, to Saturday March 8.

The publicity poster for my "I've Got to Sing a Torch Song" performances in March 1986 at the Studio (Nathan Cohen) Theatre in Toronto captured just what I was trying to portray on stage.

The YPT staff looked after all the details, producing a wonderful poster in the style of the 1940s, and seeing to handbills, tickets, staging, tuning the piano, and ordering in the fire marshal, although I had to pay for him. All I had to think about was what to wear. What would a torch singer wear? I looked through the CBC TV costume department's wonderful collection, including nineteenth-century hats with feathers, shiny golden shoes, feather boas, mink stoles and sequined chiffon dresses from the 1930s. The helpful staff there brought out a long gold lamé dress and a black sequined jacket – the perfect outfit for a nightclub chanteuse. The dress was formfitting but not too tight and had a bit of a swish around the hem so I could wander around the stage, perhaps with a drink in hand. When I asked what the fitting, the jacket, the dress, the gold shoes would cost, I was told there was no charge. I almost kissed them, but they said *Torch Song* sounded like a fine idea, and they were happy to help. I did kiss them when I came by to pick up the outfit and all the accessories.

By now word of my enterprise had made it to the CBC announce staff, and some of the senior announcers were not enthusiastic. They included my supervisor, who called me into his tiny office for a "chat." He claimed that if all CBC staff announcers started doing freelance work, especially theatrical work, it would bring the CBC into disrepute. "Where will it end?" he asked. "Requests for overtime jobs? Absenteeism?" I explained I wasn't doing this show for fame or fortune, and it was costing me money. He took that as even greater evidence of my foolishness. I explained it was a creative effort I'd dreamed of doing since I was a teenager, and that a CBC announcer singing on stage might even reflect well on the corporation. And, besides, I said, the story of my torch singers fitted well with "Listen to the Music." He was not persuaded. The petty, negative attitude, which was typical of my male colleagues, was hurtful, and none of them came to the show. It also undermined my confidence.

The closer opening night came, the more anxious I became and the less certain I was doing the right thing. What was I thinking? A one-woman show in Toronto? This wasn't Four Corners, Ontario. I couldn't sleep and lay awake for hours asking myself why I kept putting myself in situations of extreme stress, like reading the TV news.

You would think by now I'd know better than to overextend myself. But it was too late to cancel. A couple of weeks before the show, posters showed up all over town. There were advertisements in the major papers. There was no turning back. I had lost control of this nerve-racking undertaking. Then the day before opening night I could feel a head-cold coming on, which happened every time I sang in public or took a voice exam. It only increased my anxiety.

On opening night, the theatre was sold out. We had rehearsed for two weeks there, so I was familiar with the stage and my props: two champagne glasses on the piano and a black stool for me to drape myself around. At 8:00 p.m., Norm Abbott, who I'd never seen wear anything but jeans, arrived, looking stylish in a dress suit, complete with a black tie and carnation. I was wearing the gold lamé dress. We stood in the wings waiting for the lights to dim. In those final seconds I started to feel lightheaded. The stage director pointed at us. We walked out on stage. I peered into the lights and think I saw people in the front rows smiling. Then I heard the audience applaud and all my anxiety evaporated.

We made our way through the whole program. The first vocals were somewhat shaky especially when I had to sing in a higher register. My voice telling the story of these women was steadier. The critics were there and apparently most of them liked the idea. The next morning some of the headlines read: "Pacsu keeps the Torch Burning," "Torch song, Pacsu's Living Fantasy." One critic was negative: "Torch Singer Lacks a Steady Flame." He was probably right about that, but another wrote "Radio's Velvet Voice Got It Right." Overall, theatre critics liked the sincerity of the presentation and considered it a worthwhile effort. The opening night was by far the most nerve-racking and, as the days went by, I relaxed, and toward the end almost began to enjoy myself. The little theatre was sold out every night.

After the show's week-long run, my CBC supervisor called me into his office again. There were no congratulations, no "Nice work

Margaret, we're proud of you." Nothing like that, not even hello. He looked at me then at the small chair pushed against his desk. I sat in it. "Well, Margaret," he began. "There will be no penalty this time." Penalty? He looked past me at the door. "Management would prefer you to keep this kind of thing to a one-time project," he said. It's not often, perhaps unfortunately, that I keep my mouth shut, but this time I did. He stood up. Meeting over.

One positive result of the show was meeting an older man named Gerry Gest, who until recently had managed a band devoted to the repertoire of the 1930s and 1940s. He asked me to join a small group of musicians who performed music from this era around town. Naturally, I said yes. There were a few musicians in among them who were not wholly committed to the music of this period, but eventually I sorted out those who had my musical taste, were willing to rehearse new arrangements and felt comfortable working together. Our band needed a name, and we came up with the Orange Blossom Orchestra which had a nostalgic ring to it.

Singing in The Orange Blossom Orchestra was a delight. What could be more fun than wearing vintage gowns and singing old songs? There were three or four or sometimes five of us and we played at Casa Loma and the McMichael Gallery, as well as clubs and restaurants around Toronto.

The band included pianist Jordan Klapman, who liked to play the music of Fats Waller, the renowned jazz pianist of the thirties and forties. Tony Quarrington, a splendid musician and professional guitar player made the arrangements for our group and transcribed many of the songs into my key. There was a drummer on occasion and a bass player, a tall fellow who looked just like his lofty instrument and, best of all, a tuba player. That was an obligatory instrument in marching bands in the old days and in dance bands before bass players took over.

After sitting on the stairs watching band rehearsals, Andrew said he wanted a tuba for Christmas. That didn't happen, but 6-year-old Andrew and his 3- year-old sister seemed to enjoy Christmas anyway.

We rehearsed at my house. We would gather in the early evening, and Andrew and Alexandra would settle on the staircase and peer down into the living room. They loved the tuba player and giggled whenever he blew his horn. Before we started, I served beer, and set up a microphone and amplifier, a used machine to help carry my voice over the band's loud volume. The musicians changed occasionally but Jordan and Tony always came.

When we took "I've Got to Sing a Torch Song" to the McMichael Gallery, they created a poster with a delightful caricature of a torch singer. (Poster courtesy of McMichael Gallery © McMichael Canadian Art Collection.)

Because the band would be paid to perform, I joined the union, the Toronto Musicians Association, Local 149, which made me feel almost professional. I still had a problem remembering words, so I always took a music stand to keep the sheet music in front of me. Gerry, who became our manager, found us jobs in unusual places, and one of our first gigs took place in the conservatory of Casa Loma, the faux castle built just before the First World War on a hill overlooking downtown Toronto. It was the perfect setting for our kind of music. The airy space was filled with flowers, although there were no orange blossoms, and despite the numerous tables and chairs, the audience found room to dance. We played at Berlin's on Yonge Street, a real nightclub where people dressed in period clothing danced to our melodies. Another delightful venue we played was the McMichael, the art gallery just outside of Toronto in Kleinberg. It is built into the side of a heavily forested valley and contains numerous works by the Group of Seven. Many of these artists studied in France during the Impressionist period I love so much, and their paintings brought back memories of the days I spent in Aix-en-Provence looking for the landscapes Cezanne captured. It was a stunning setting in which to play our kind of music. I performed there on several occasions as the singer in a trio – me, piano and guitar –as well as with the full Orange Blossom Orchestra. On one occasion an outstanding young Toronto trumpet player joined us. His solo was so compelling that instead of coming in for the last sixteen bars, I just listened. He finished up the piece and received the applause he deserved, from the audience and from all of us in the band.

Another Toronto group, which had been around for a while playing nostalgic society music, had been offered a spot at the Canadian National Exhibition that takes place in Toronto at the end of the summer. Their singer was a handsome young crooner with a warm baritone sound, but the band leader thought a female voice would add some variety and approached me about occasional appearances. I didn't know any of the musicians, but we had several rehearsals, they were friendly, their music was familiar, and we sounded professional. One evening, I noticed a crowd of people surrounding an elegant looking man. It was Bill Cosby, the now disgraced American comedian and actor, who was appearing at the Ex that year. During an intermission, I introduced myself, and we talked about New Jersey and coming to Canada. He was cheerful and pleasant, and told me he had been to Toronto several times. He found Canadians very polite, but he wouldn't want to live here permanently.

We gradually added more music, still primarily from the 1930s and 1940s, to the Orange Blossom repertoire, and to our amazement CBC even interviewed us. A positive outcome for me was finding a teacher, David Clenman, who helped me position my voice correctly. I had started out as a soprano, moved down to a mezzo-soprano, but David placed my voice an octave lower. I could at last sing without straining my vocal cords, and for longer. It gave my spoken voice a softer, more mellow quality, which a friend suggested might lull my radio listeners to sleep. At least it didn't awake further opposition from the announce office.

Our band continued until the death of manager Gerry Gest. Without his efforts at booking our gigs we gradually drifted apart. I am very proud of the musicians who backed me over those years in the Orange Blossom Orchestra.

Chapter 17

The road opens to "Easy Street"

By June 1987, Fredd and I had been doing "Listen to the Music" five nights a week for twelve years. It was such a familiar and well-liked part of the stereo schedule that the music department managers paid us little attention. We came in every day, sat in Freddie's cramped office, and produced ninety minutes of programming. We pretty much stayed out of the way, and everyone in the department went about their business around us. Which is why I was startled when one afternoon the head of the department jumped out of his office, stood in my path and asked if I had a minute. He gestured me into his office and closed the door. Never a good sign, although this time it was. "Margaret," he said, "we would like you to host a new jazz program every evening, if you are interested."

Of course I was, but the invitation didn't come as a complete surprise. Eitan Cornfield and I had already cracked open the door to jazz at the CBC. I got to know Eitan, who produced a weekly classical music program, when he filled in for a few weeks on "Listen to the Music" while Fredd was on holiday. Over a cup of coffee one day while preparing the show we discovered we were both closeted jazz fans. Eitan was a cellist, loved classical music, but had grown up listening to jazz, real jazz: Miles Davis, Charlie Parker, Oscar Peterson, and Chet Baker. I told him about my love of jazz and enthusiasm for Chet. It was fun, and when we were off the air we talked more about jazz than classical music. What focused the conversation was the music department saying they needed a daily summer replacement program. Did anyone have any ideas? Well, yes, we did. Over the next few days and with the help of lots more coffee, we developed a show called "Easy Street." We came up with themes, blocked out a couple of sample programs and submitted the idea with little expectation it would be accepted. It seemed like too much fun. But amazingly, we were wrong. "Easy Street" went on the air for an hour every weekday starting at 10 p.m. It was not prime time, but we were sure Canadians who shared our love of jazz would find us, and they did. We had a good time with the program over the summer, playing our favourite music, although every time we played Chet Baker, Eitan pointed out I was swooning like most of Chet's female fans – not something the music department managers would approve of, he thought.

But if they heard my enthusiasm, it didn't bother them. And so it was after a couple of months on the air that I was being asked if I was interested in continuing our program. The department wanted to extend "Easy Street" for a year.

Not wanting to jump across his desk and yell "Yes! Yes!" I said, "Well, let me ask Eitan." A jazz program for a year! I tried not to run down the hall to his office. When I told him, he was as excited as I was. But this was the music department, where enthusiasm was often used as a lever of control, so we pretended to hesitate, then with feigned reluctance said yes. As for my work schedule, with "Listen to the Music" this meant my being on air for two and a half hours a day. A tiring amount of time. But "Easy Street" with its mix of pre-1960s jazz, anecdotes, and well-researched profiles of the musicians, never felt like work. Both Eitan and I thought it was a dream come true. We knew the musicians of this era were a peculiar group. Because they'd focused on their music at the expense of the rest of their lives, the stories about them were compelling. "Easy Street," we figured, was the perfect platform to tell them.

It was a good year. As it turned out, we rode what seemed like a surge of new interest in jazz. And we had the resources of the superb CBC record library, which had a vast collection of LPs and 78s and even some old glass discs all carefully listed on well-thumbed cards stored in rows of wooden filing drawers. To separate serious users from those looking for party music, the library's holdings were listed with an alpha-numeric coding system. Still, even mastering the code wasn't a guarantee of success. All too frequently we would find a rare 78 recording in the card file, only to discover its sleeve was empty.

Many of the singers and musicians of the be-bop era that "Easy Street" featured were by now quite old. This meant we usually had at least one obituary a week to research. In a way, that made our job easier, if we could find information in the CBC library related to the artist. This was before the internet, of course, when research meant looking in reference books or clipping files. Fortunately, just as we started our series, the renewed interest in jazz had led to new scholarship and the re-issue and re-mastering of older recordings in a CD format. It was an exciting time for jazz lovers, and we tried to reflect that excitement in the program.

I loved "Easy Street," and so did our listeners. But popularity didn't mean much to CBC. In one of its regular upheavals, CBC Radio management decided that jazz wasn't really music. Classical music was the only true form. There was no room for "Easy Street" along side Mozart. The hosts, producers, researchers and all the others who worked on these variety programs were lumped in with rock 'n' roll and other forms of pop music in a sort of catchall department for comedy programs, quiz shows and other endeavours that weren't classical music or news.

Following the machinations of CBC management could be a full-time job, and not one I was interested in. So I was surprised and unsure what to expect when I found a note in my in-box one morning asking me to see a new manager, new to me anyway, later that afternoon. Things began well enough with him telling me how pleased he was with "Easy Street" and the great music we played, and what a wonderful program it was. All of which made me a little uneasy. He went on to talk glowingly about the benefits of re-organization and the vital part "Easy Street" would play in the new department. By then I knew this was going somewhere I wouldn't like, and it did.

"So," he finally said, "we'd really love you to continuing hosting the program, and I'm sure you want to continue, but as it turns out the only way we can do that is if you go on contract." I must have looked surprised and disappointed because he quickly added "Of course, you could stay on as a staff announcer with "Listen to the Music" but then we would have to find another host for 'Easy Street.'"

It wasn't much of a choice at all. In effect, I was being laid off. I either had to leave my staff position as host of "Listen to the Music" or say goodbye to "Easy Street." As a staff announcer I was in a union and had some protection from management's air-headed and sometimes vindictive decisions. I also had a pension. On contract, I would have nothing. Management could refuse to renew my contract at any time and on a whim. Still, considering the program's popularity, I thought it improbable I would be let go soon. On the other hand, I was growing weary of doing two and a half hours of programming every day. On contract that would be cut to an hour of programming I loved. In the end, I decided to give up my job security and seniority of almost two decades and chose an uncertain freelance life with "Easy Street."

An "Easy Street" publicity postcard. It took a while to reach "Easy Street," with detours through Princeton, Paris and Cincinnati, but the end was well worth the time it took. (Post card courtesy of CBC).

The program was becoming what we had hoped for, a kind of late-evening nightclub, with all kinds of interesting people dropping by. Early on a listener sent us a tape made by RCA Victor on July 30, 1942, two days before the start of the American Federation of Musician's strike banning union musicians from making commercial recordings. It was Fats Waller's last commercial release: "That's What the Well-dressed Man in Harlem Will Wear." We used it on several occasions as an alternative theme. Not all our choices were that successful, and some baffled our listeners. A track by Ken Nordine, a popular voice actor in the Chicago area in the 1940s, was among them. In the late 1950s he recorded several albums of what he called word jazz, a kind of free-flowing verbal riff, a stream-of-consciousness poetry, with a swinging musical background by the Fred Katz Group. Our listeners' reaction was: What was that all about? We didn't have an answer, so we set Mr. Nordine aside. That was typical of our response to listeners, who didn't hesitate to tell us what they liked and what they thought about our choices. Several older listeners who had seen Thelonious Monk and Clifford Brown perform live at Birdland in New York wrote in detail about their experience. There were inspiring letters from college students expressing their awe at hearing the young Wynton Marsalis for the first time. And there were a great many listeners who said they never got enough of Ella and Billie.

One listener sent us an extraordinary cassette tape entitled, perhaps aptly, "Mean Mothers," of early blues singers dating from 1926. I had never heard of most of these women on the tape, singers who should have been much better known than they were. From then on, we featured many of them, Mamie Smith, for example. In 1920 she became the first Black singer to record with the record label OKeh. "Crazy Blues" was on one side and "Right Here for You" on the other. It sold an astonishing 75,000 copies to a Black audience in the first month it was released. Black newspapers like the *Chicago Defender* began to advertise recordings to their readers. Labels like OKeh, which originally marketed to white audiences, realized the growing appeal of Black artists to a white public. They sent scouts to the American South to search for blues singers and offer one-time deals. No long-term contracts. They discovered several female blues singers who wrote fresh and feisty songs with raw vocals, never portraying themselves as victims.

Rosetta Reitz, an American feminist and jazz historian, was the inspiration behind the 1970s re-release of early blues recordings. She founded Rosetta Records and with considerable difficulty collected old 78s and remastered their uneven sound. The "Mean Mothers" tape sent to us by the listener was dubbed from a 1980 Rosetta LP, *Independent Women's Blues Vol. I*. We didn't recognize many of the singers names, but their talent shone through. They have beautiful deep voices and express heartfelt emotions, as the song titles show. Just listen to Bessie Brown ("Ain't Much Good in the Best of Men Nowadays," 1928), Harlem Hannah ("Keep your Nose Out of Mama's Business," 1933) and Blu Lu Barker ("I Don't Dig You Jack"). There's more, Maggie Jones ("You Ain't Gonna Feed in My Pasture Now," 1926), Rosa Henderson ("Can't be Bothered with No

Sheik," 1931), Mary Dixon ("You Can't Sleep in My Bed," 1929), and Ida Cox ("One Hour Mama," 1939). These women expressed their own sexuality and did it with humour. One anonymous writer put it this way: "It is funny, sad, moving, empowering and it's beautiful music too. It evokes hope and strength the only way blues can do, by lifting us up with expressive songs that echo their pain. There is wit and brashness in the songs about women's role and position in society."

As brilliant as this music is, it was difficult to find out much about many of these women, their lives and even how and where they recorded their songs. Did they sing in church choirs? Did they train their voices at all? How were they recorded at the time, in studios, backrooms and who were the technicians? Did they write their own blues songs or was there a cadre of even lesser-known song writers? How were they paid, by the record, with contracts? We couldn't find the answers to these and many more questions about these extraordinarily talented women.

The CBC did promote "Easy Street" and once asked Ted Michener, a well-known Toronto cartoonist and artist, to draw a caricature for a program promotion in CBC's Radio Guide. *(Courtesy of CBC).*

Listeners sent more than CDs and suggestions, though. Occasionally, we'd get a box of cookies or a piece of fruit cake along with the thanks and warm regards. This was at a time when we happily wolfed down whatever had arrived with no concern at all that someone might have sent it with ill intent. My favorite gift came from a motorcycle gang in British Columbia whose members wrote to us all the time with requests and intelligent comments on our choice of music. One day the CBC mailman left a book-sized package in my announce office pigeon-hole. I picked it up with other mail on my way out of the office. Curious about what was in it, I stopped in the parking lot next to the Jarvis Street building to open it. Peter Gzowski just happened to be walking out of the radio building at the end of that day's "This Country in the Morning" at the same time. Peter and I didn't meet all that often, largely because our shifts were different and our studios at opposite ends of the building. But we chatted that morning and as I opened the package, I told him about our biker fans in British Columbia. It took a bit of effort to peel off several layers of tape and paper, but inside was a small white cardboard box. And inside that were a dozen little joints with their twisted ends poking up against a layer of Saran wrap. I looked at him and he looked at me. This, of course, was at a time when the mere possession of marijuana could mean jail. "What a lucky girl," he mumbled as he slouched off to the Red Lion across the road. Eitan looked pleased when I showed him our gift. He took half and I took the other half home for Bob. After all, he had been to Woodstock and knew what to do with them.

Eitan and I often featured Canadian jazz musicians, including Moe Koffman, Rob McConnell, and of course guitarist Ed Bickert, whose recording of "Easy Street," written by Alan Rankin Jones in 1940, opened and closed our show almost every night for years. It had been recorded by Duke Ellington, June Christy, and Stan Kenton in 1951. Louis Armstrong and Jack Teagarden, among many others, also had a version. Theme music is supposed to be consistent, but so many wonderful musicians had recorded the song over the years that occasionally we slipped in a different version to the delight of our listeners.

Choosing selections for jazz afficionados was tricky because many of them knew the music and musicians who played it better than Eitan and I did. And if we made a mistake, they were quick to tell us.

The most embarrassing one was when we announced the death of Canadian jazz singer Anne Marie Moss and broadcast a carefully researched obituary. She was a well-liked musician, who had a good sense of humour. We discovered that the day after we broadcast the obituary when Eitan received a phone call from a pleasant-sounding woman who said she often listened to our program and enjoyed it. He was expecting a request for a favourite piece of music and was surprised –falling off the chair surprised – when she said her name was Anne Marie Moss and wanted to assure us that she wasn't dead. While she anticipated our obit could mean a welcome spike in CD sales, she asked if we would please make a correction to assure her family and friends that she wasn't dead, at least not yet. We did, along with our apologies, managing to put another program together featuring her music.

Another time, we introduced a recording by pianist Marian McPartland, who had played at the Hickory House on 52nd St. in New York between 1952 and 1962. We talked a bit about her background and the musicians in her group, including her long-time drummer. The problem was he wasn't her long-time drummer, in fact he had never played with her, and as we later found out quite possibly didn't even like her. It wasn't long after we had named him that the calls began and then the letters. No. He wasn't her drummer. Her drummer was Joe Morello who played with her for years. Embarrassing? Of course. But the good thing was that there was enough information to put together a whole program about Morello and Marian.

Marian McPartland was an accomplished jazz pianist and composer. She was also a warm and funny person. We met when she was in Toronto to record a program for National Public Radio, and we went on to continue our friendship. (Photo courtesy of CBC).

Born and trained in Britain, as an adult McPartland had an outstanding career in the United States. In addition to playing with many well-known American jazz musicians at the Hickory House over the years, she started her own record label and hosted "Piano Jazz" on

National Public Radio. Every week for an astonishing thirty-three years, from 1978 to 2011, she showcased some of the best jazz music in the world. She received many awards for her work, including in 2010 the Order of the British Empire. I met her at CBC Toronto when she was in town for a few days to record a program for NPR. Eitan, who helped produce that program, introduced us and we soon found ourselves deep in conversation, exchanging jazz stories. She was a very funny, charming woman, who in the 1980s wrote about being one of the few women instrumentalists in jazz. "Can't we women make our own contribution to jazz by playing like women," she asked, "but still capturing the essential elements of jazz – good beat, good ideas, honesty and true feelings?" It was this outlook on life that made the two of us click and we became good friends.

Marian came back to Toronto a few months later to play at the Senator, a noted local jazz club. The place was packed. I called her often at her home in Port Washington, on Long Island, and we talked about everything, including her youth in England, where she studied classical music before turning to jazz. I told her about my mother's music career. She almost took that route, she said, and her parents hoped she would play Mozart rather than Thelonious Monk. She told me a little about her famous cornet player husband, Jimmy McPartland. They had met and married in Belgium at the end of World War Two. At their return to the States Marian had played in the Big Bands and Dixie groups with Jimmy but gradually by the 1950's she was lured by the siren sounds of bop and cool jazz. Jimmy and Marian always remained friends and played together often. But in 1970 they divorced. Their friendship lasted over the years and in 1991 they remarried a few weeks before Jimmy's death. He died on March 13, two days before his 84th birthday. She never really loved anyone else she told me. Marian died at the age of ninety-eight in 2013. It was painful to lose her.

I've talked with a lot of musicians over the years, and some of those conversations have stayed with me. I did a telephone interview with Oscar Peterson in the late 1980s. I was very nervous, but he wasn't. He had performed on stage, done enough interviews, and hosted enough television shows over the years that he was a pro and quickly put me at ease. He answered all my questions about his musical family and his early training in Montreal. He said his father, Daniel Peterson, had taught himself music from books and a collapsible organ when he was in the merchant navy. His mother, Kathleen, came from a highly musical family, and his sister, Daisy Peterson Sweeny, who was a well-respected piano teacher, helped him greatly. All this led him to have the technique of a classical pianist, which was unusual among jazz musicians in both Europe and North America.

He said he knew his "Hymn to Freedom" had become one of the crusading compositions that inspired the civil rights movement in the United States. He was just as proud of his *Canadiana Suite*, with passages called "Land of the Misty Giants" and "Laurentide Blues." I asked him about the school he'd once opened in Toronto to teach jazz – the Advanced School of Contemporary Music. He explained he'd had to close it in 1964 as he was getting older and, sadly, could no longer fit in his concerts and other commitments with teaching. I did tell him that whenever I heard the first few bars of a piece he played, I recognized him immediately. His style was always elegant and technically amazing. He was very gracious, mentioning Norman Granz, who had introduced him in New York City in 1949 at a Jazz at the Philharmonic concert at Carnegie Hall. Granz remained his manager for most of his career and a champion of racial equality. I wanted to talk about some of his musical friends and colleagues: Ella Fitzgerald, Dizzy Gillespie, Lester Young but we ran out of time. I managed to squeeze in that while I was growing up in New Jersey I'd always thought he was a Yankee, but now that I had lived in Canada for many years, I was so proud he'd never left. We finished the program with music from the Oscar Peterson Trio's legendary recording "Live at the Blue Note," with guitarist Herb Ellis and bassist Ray Brown, and a tune sung by Ella Fitzgerald with Oscar playing a quiet, contemplative accompaniment.

I talked with him again a few years later at one of the most amazing and moving performances I've ever been part of. On May 10, 1993, in the Glenn Gould Studio in the new CBC building on Front St., Oscar Peterson was awarded the Glenn Gould Prize of $50,000. He was just the third person to receive this award. The program was broadcast on CBC Stereo, and I presented the event from the stage. The original plan was straightforward. I would introduce him, Oscar would play a couple of selections and then receive the award from Governor General Ray Hnatyshn. I would stand at a lectern across the platform from Oscar, who would be seated at the piano.

It all seemed simple enough, but two days before the scheduled ceremony, Oscar had a stroke. His left side was paralyzed. His agent called with the terrible news. He wouldn't be able to come to the presentation. With all the arrangements already made and invitations sent out, we decided to go ahead with a brief ceremony anyway, only without Oscar. The next day, the day before the presentation, his agent called again, this time to say Oscar would be there. He didn't want to disappoint us or his public. We planned several ways we could do the program, not knowing what to expect.

That evening, right on time, Oscar arrived on the stage in a wheelchair. His assistant pushed him over to the Steinway. After greeting the cheering crowd, incredibly he began to play. From where I was standing on the other side of the stage, I could see he kept his left hand in his lap, and played everything with his right hand, even exacting, virtuoso pieces. The way the piano was placed, the audience could not see clearly that he was using only his right hand. He paused for a few minutes between numbers while the audience applauded, but he kept on playing for what must have been forty minutes. When he finally put his right hand down and turned to face the hall, the audience rose as one, applauding and cheering this artist who had just executed a superhuman feat. None of us there that evening would ever forget it. His friend, the Canadian politician and amateur pianist

Bob Rae, said a one-handed Oscar was better than just about anyone with two hands. It took almost two years of therapy before Oscar played in public again.

"Easy Street" was a different experience for me than any other program in my twenty-two years at CBC. Both Eitan and I had a rapport with the audience that was truly personal. Many of our listeners had grown up at the same time as us, so we were playing the wonderful jazz music of our youth in the 1950s and did so for seven wonderful years. Toward its end, Eitan, my original producer, was assigned to new projects, but Diane English, a young woman with a remarkable knowledge and affection for jazz, took over. But "Easy Street" came to an end on August 28, 1994. It was not my choice, although incredibly management claimed that I had asked to leave the program. This was not true. We knew trouble was on the horizon when the program was rescheduled from nightly broadcasts to two hours only on Sunday nights and then finally to two hours on Sunday afternoons, a dead spot in the radio schedule. My contract was reduced accordingly. CBC Radio was once again heading in a different direction at the whim of a new head of the radio variety department and, for reasons obscure to me, "Easy Street" was not in their plan. It was an ill thought-out and painful decision, not only for me personally but for our listeners, who were never told why we disappeared from the airwaves.

"Easy Street" did give Diane and I a final moment of pleasure – selecting the music for the final two-hour program. It was difficult, and we had asked our faithful listeners to help by sending us a list of their favorite jazz artists. We were overwhelmed by the response. It would probably have taken another seven years to play all the requests. But we didn't just want to present random selections. We could fit perhaps twenty pieces into those two hours. So, with help from our audience, we decided to pick the emblematic music of three periods: Early jazz and Boogie Woogie, big bands and their singers from the 1930s to the early 1950s, and finally the mellow sound of bebop in the 1960s and 1970s.

We chose some amazing and wonderful music that night, but before we faded away there had to be that final memorable one that personified the sweet sounds heard on "Easy Street." It seemed fitting that it was the most chosen work by our audience. More listeners had asked for Miles Davis's "Kind of Blue" than any other jazz disc, and it was at the top of my list and Diane's as well. It's not only the musicians that make this record great, but also the innovative music. Miles and company take us somewhere new, with sounds of modal jazz and it remains as exciting now as it was in 1959. We played "So What," featuring Davis, John Coltrane, Cannonball Adderley, Paul Chambers, Jimmy Cobb, Bill Evans all together on this great jazz recording.

After seven years on the radio, 1,800 hours of programming and more than 20,000 pieces of the sweetest sounds we could find. I signed off for the last time: "Unfortunately, I can see that stop sign ahead which means we have finally come to the end of 'Easy Street.' There are so many people to thank but most of all my producers, Diane English, and Eitan Cornfield, who originated this program and of course all of you who joined us over the years. It's been a blast, so if you believe hard enough and keep on swinging...."

Chapter 18

Kurt Vonnegut car salesman

"Easy Street" was over, but not my freelance contract with CBC, nor the severe mood swings that kept me up during the day and made me crash every evening. They were as bad as ever, putting a terrible strain both on me and my family. Being shuffled out of "Easy Street" did not help. What was happening now was far beyond having good days and bad days. I was in trouble, and I knew it.

I looked for help and, with fortune smiling on me, I found it in Dr. Cy Marks, a psychiatrist and hypnotherapist, who used relaxation techniques to help patients with serious mood disorders. I explained I was fifty-six years old, moody, was having hot flashes and the physical changes of menopause. My son was thirteen, my daughter nine and my husband Bob, was singlehandedly holding the family together. I also told him about my mother's mood swings and occasional flakiness, as well as my grandmother's odd violent conduct. I said I was sure being Hungarian went some way to explain what I was experiencing. Dr. Marks initially agreed with me, but after listening to this thesis longer than it deserved, he felt being Hungarian was an insufficient explanation for my mercurial behaviour. He suggested hypnotherapy would be effective and produce results more quickly than psychotherapy. I was doubtful, finally agreeing only after he promised not to make me cluck like a chicken or roll over on the floor like a dog while I was hypnotized.

Dr. Marks hypnotized me several times, but it made no difference. He then suggested the problem could be bipolar disorder, and that lithium might minimize the symptoms. His diagnosis frightened me. He was talking about what we used to call manic depression, the kind of disorder one's dotty old auntie had, the one who ended up in an asylum, never to be heard from again. Or the fellow who in a manic phase, flew to India, paid $25,000 for an elephant and had it shipped back to Toronto for his children. I didn't think I would ever buy elephants or tigers, and I didn't embrace Dr. Marks' diagnosis. I said I needed to think about it but had no intention of going along with his suggested treatment. Of course I talked to Bob about it when I got home, and he urged me to give lithium a try. My mood swings had become much more frequent and much deeper, and they were making life truly difficult for him, the last person I wanted to hurt. I decided that for his and the children's sake, I had to do something, so I went back to the doctor for a prescription.

On June 11, 1994, with my first bottle of lithium in hand, I took the subway down to the Eaton Centre, ordered a bacon, lettuce and tomato sandwich, coffee, and a glass of water from a stand in the food court, and took the first dose of what has now been my companion for thirty years. Almost immediately it seemed as if little gates blocked my mood from swinging too high or too low. I was astonished. I had always thought that I should be able to control my moods through willpower alone, and that it was my fault that I no longer could do so. I had never seriously considered that there might be something wrong with my brain chemistry that could be ameliorated, if not entirely fixed. The doctor was pleased and soon figured out the correct dosage. There were side effects, mostly dehydration, but without this wondrous drug, Bob and I and the children would not have survived as a family. My only regret is that I wasn't diagnosed and prescribed lithium sooner.

It was around this time that I realized my days at CBC were coming to an end. I'd worked there for twenty-two years. That was a long time, and, in a way, I was sorry to leave, but on the other hand it felt right.

My final program for CBC was a thirteen-week series of live concerts entitled "On Stage at the Glenn Gould Studio," scheduled to begin on February 5, 1995. It would be broadcast on both CBC radio networks. My role was simple: to introduce Canada's pre-eminent female opera singer, Maureen Forrester, who would host two-hour concerts by some of the country's best-known musicians, including pianist Angela Hewitt, guitarist Liona Boyd, Canadian Brass, and the Barra MacNeils.

Canadian operatic contralto Maureen Forrester and I co-hosted "On Stage," a 1995 CBC Radio music series. We laughed a lot working together, particularly about our unruly curls. (Photo courtesy of CBC).

I had never met Maureen Forrester but knew her reputation as one of the great contraltos of our time. Her unique voice ranged from soprano to tenor and was immediately recognizable, like the sound of Oscar Peterson's jazz piano or Glenn's recordings. I met her at our first rehearsal, and we got along well from the start. She was very friendly and eager to talk about her children and asked me about mine. We laughed a lot. We discovered we both loved clothes, although hers were out of my price range. We had the same kind of problems with our curly hair. It tended to look disheveled, but that, she assured me, was part of our charm.

The thirteen-week series started well. The idea was that I would introduce Maureen to the audience, she would speak briefly about that week's performers, and then we would leave the stage and sit in the wings. At some point, Maureen would slip away, and I would thank the audience and the artists at the end of the concert. As enjoyable as it was, my role was expendable and after a few weeks it began to puzzle me. I asked the producer why I was there when Maureen could just as easily do the brief openings and closings herself. The producer looked away in silence, and then down, eventually saying that I was there "just in case."

"Just in case of what?" I asked. There didn't seem to be any difficulties, at least none that I saw. Maureen and I got along well. I enjoyed her company and her stories, and she appeared to feel the same way about me.

"No, no, nothing to do with you," the producer hastened to say. "It's, uh, a health issue."

"What kind of health issue?" I asked, imagining Maureen collapsing in the middle of the live session and ambulances and …

The producer, a pleasant young woman, obviously feeling uncomfortable talking about it, finally said that sometimes Miss Forrester, well, drank too much alcohol and would forget what she had scheduled that day. And sometimes she wasn't entirely sure about dates, and they were afraid she might forget to come to the Glenn Gould Studio.

I thanked her, at least understanding her concern, although my experience over the past weeks made it hard for me to believe.

But then, on one Sunday afternoon, midway through the series, the time came and went for the audio check and the run-through of her script and Maureen wasn't there, nor was she answering her phone. The young producer was worried. She told me to prepare to do the program alone. A production assistant took a taxi to Maureen's home, pounded on the door, and found her sleepy but capable of hurriedly putting on her clothes, as she continued to do as the taxi raced back downtown. It was a near thing, but she made it in time, walked out on stage and introduced the guest artist. That was the closest we came to a mishap. We finished the series without further incident.

I saw her occasionally after that, but she did fewer public engagements and eventually retired from performing. It wasn't until she died in a nursing home in 2010 that I learned she'd also been suffering from dementia and not just a drinking problem. Her death was a great loss to all of us. Maureen Forrester remains one of Canada's preeminent artists.

In May 1995, I was ready to stop working at CBC, but I wasn't ready to stop working altogether. Being on staff for all those years had given me wonderful experiences but had severely limited my access to outside projects. That door was about to open. To take advantage of it, I knew I needed the one person every actor and performer I'd ever met seemed to have: an agent. I'd seen the movie. If I didn't have one, how could I possibly jump in the taxi, turn my head and yell, "Call my agent!" The problem was where to find one and how to know if he or she was an appropriate choice. It's never easy. You are looking for someone who understands you, knows your strengths, who sends you out for suitable auditions, and who will back you up in case of conflict with the production people.

I signed on with Gerry Jordan, proprietor and sole employee of Jordan and Associates Talent Management. His office was then on Yonge Street, and the moment I walked in I knew I was in the right place. There was Toronto Blue Jays memorabilia everywhere – caps, photos, autographed baseballs. I told him about my twelve-year-old son, Andrew, a Blue Jay fanatic, and the many games we went to. Then I mentioned I was a Brooklyn Dodgers fan back in the 1950s. Gerry had never met anyone who knew much about the Dodgers, and he listened to my recalling the New York Giants 3rd baseman Bobby Thomson hitting the "shot heard round the world" on October 3, 1951, ending the Dodgers' hope for a World Series role. We had a splendid conversation and eventually I gave him my CV. He took one look and said he would like to sign me on to his list of actors. From then on, he stood by me, giving me useful information about up-coming auditions, which directors were difficult to work with, and when to keep quiet. He rewrote my CV, starting it with the defining message: "Margaret Pacsu has worked extensively in the cultural arts for many years. She has hosted many functions such as the International Economic Summit introducing President and Mrs. Ronald Reagan, the Chalmers Awards, and numerous bilingual events on CBC." And it worked. Thanks to Gerry I did voice-overs for film and television documentaries, among them for Hawker Siddeley, Harbourfront, the Metropolitan Opera, Air France, and Cognac Ltd. There was one documentary before I knew Gerry for which I did the voice work in 1993. It was titled *A Matter of Choice: The Story of Dr. Henry Morgentaler*, produced by Francine E. Zuckerman and Susan Murgatroyd and directed by Nancy Jackman. He was Canada's pioneering advocate for women's right to choose. I was proud of that project. It was acclaimed by feminists, and I believe welcomed by most Canadians.

TV Ontario was then and still is today a small public television operation covering the province in both French and English. I had been turned down for a job there many years ago when I first arrived in Toronto. Now Gerry found me voice-over work narrating documentaries in both languages, and I met people there who remain my good friends. It's an organization with a relaxed atmosphere, and a group of us often took part in live TV fundraising efforts. This was something new for me. I had often wondered how the people making their pitch for our money managed to keep talking hour after hour. Now I knew. There's a script on the teleprompter, and talking points, but you can ad lib as you go along, and chat to the other fundraisers. It was live programming, but almost fun to do, not stressful like reading the news. On several occasions, Bruce Rogers, a former CBC announcer and a great trumpet player, and I were teamed up to solicit funds for the station. Off camera we not only had CBC gossip to discuss but the jazz world. He had his own band for many years, and he also told me about his horses and how he had to get up at 5:00 a.m. on frigid winter mornings to make sure they could breathe through their frozen nostrils. You learn new things all the time.

Gerry also found me commercial voice work. It's a different kind of job and is a fast-paced business. You may have a sixty second spot or thirty seconds or less if it is only a seven-second tag line. Advertising agencies develop the creative ideas, write the scripts then set up auditions for the performers. The actors parade in front of the agency people and in turn read the script until the agency finds the voice or look they want for the commercial.

We call these auditions "cattle calls." Among the cattle calls I went to was one for Lotto 6/49, Canada's national lottery. It was to be filmed not in wintry Niagara Falls or Banff but in sunny Fort Lauderdale, Florida. So one cold day in November a couple of dozen actors made their way to the agency's office. As requested, we were a group of men and women in the "over fifty" category and some of us knew each other well because we regularly went to the same auditions. Nobody told us to, but we women usually sat opposite the men, grey-haired and mostly overweight, on the other side of the room, as far away from us as they could get. It was like a high-school dance.

There was one woman nobody sat next to. We all knew who she was, of course, but she never acknowledged us. She was often awarded principal roles in these commercials. Then there was the redoubtable Jayne Eastwood, one of Canada's leading actresses, a delightful person who remembered everyone's name, always asked after our families, and had a joke ready to brighten our anxious wait.

At the audition for the lottery commercial, we were paired up in couples and asked to read a few lines of script. The production team was unusually relaxed. The producer was a young man wearing a cowboy hat who told jokes during the whole process. The man I was partnered with, and I laughed a lot and treated the audition as a frolic. To our astonishment, a few days later we were told we had the job. We were to portray a middle-aged couple given a cruise by our son who had won the 6/49 lottery. We flew down to Fort Lauderdale and were put up in a five-star hotel for four nights. Fort Lauderdale is a charming place, warm even in November, with an impressive beach crowded with people bathing and sunning themselves. Both the cast and crew felt as if we were the ones who had won the lottery, even though we'd never held a winning ticket. The shoot took place on an enormous cruise ship, with many hundreds of passengers three decks above us, peering down from dangerous heights at the activities. There was a swimming pool on our deck, and the director wanted a few shots of us in the pool. I am not at my most alluring in a bathing suit, but to my relief the director managed to keep most of me submerged.

I did learn one cinematic secret: many of those sunset scenes luring us to warm holiday destinations are filmed at dawn to minimize the risk of losing the shot to sundown. We had a wonderful time and a cheerful wrap party back at the hotel. We told our young producer we were ready to work with him again any time. These kinds of shoots don't always work out so agreeably, but this one did.

Another memorable job resulted from a friend telling me about an unusual new organization called Voice Print. Founded in 1990, it provided an audio-only 24/7 news broadcast on sub-channel TV for the blind and visually impaired. It now also offers video channels in French and English. When I worked there it relied entirely on volunteers – and may still do – to read the news from various newspapers and do occasional interviews. I listened to the station all one morning and was impressed by how professional it sounded. Gerry had heard about it and said they might be pleased to have one more news reader on board. So I called them and was invited to audition.

Voice Print's office in Toronto was unlike any I have ever worked in. It had waist-high railings for employees to use as a guide between the front office door and their workspace. All the desks had the latest in Braille typewriters and phones with raised dots on the keys. The few sighted management people showed me around the workstations and introduced me to two audio producers who were partially sighted but seemed to get around with considerable ease. Soon, I was shaking hands with two technicians, both blind, each in his own recording studio. I had no idea how this audio tryout was going to take place. Tony, one of the technicians, explained he would be recording the news as I read it, and just to take it easy and relax. I did a good job, so he told me afterward, although there was a slight hesitation on the pronunciation of Kuala Lumpur. Did I want to do a retake?

Within two days someone called and offered me a position Monday mornings recording the ten o'clock international news. I was glad to find that Tony would be the engineer. He was probably the best technician I ever worked with. He heard every breath, every sigh, the slightest sibilance. He and I worked together happily for several years. I asked him on occasion what it was like to be blind. He was candid about his experiences. For example, in the morning his wife walked with him to the bus stop, and in the afternoon the bus driver always waited until he reached the door and climbed aboard. Voice Print later went on to bigger things, a TV channel of its own, with interviews and programming appealing not just to the blind but to anyone unable to read newspapers and magazines for whatever reason.

Gerry managed to find me work on an odd assortment of commercials during the years I volunteered at Voice Print. For one of them the producer wanted me to dye my hair red. I hesitated. It's easy, they said. It'll wash right out. Three months later my hair was still a dirty brick colour that looked, well, like a bad dye job. Eventually it grew out, but I've never let anyone with a dye pot near my tresses again.

For another assignment I played the role of a surly, middle-aged cashier in a bookstore. When I read it, the script and stage directions left me puzzled. It was a commercial for cars, and I couldn't see how selling cars was connected to a surly cashier. But Gerry said I'd find it an interesting job, and I believed him. It was shot on a beautiful sunny November day in 2002 in an old store crowded to the ceiling with books on sagging shelves. The film company had rented the location in a small town just north of Toronto. Once I arrived, the wardrobe person pulled out a drab brown suit and showed me where to change. I hated the suit almost as much as the dusting of mousey makeup she applied. It made me look dowdy, but that's what the director wanted. A handsome young man escorted me "on set," showed me to a chair behind the cash register and told me I might as well sit down since it would be a while before the shoot began. He was right, but eventually the director came by, introduced himself, and explained the action. A customer would walk up to the cashier (me) and hold out money. All I had to do was take the money, give him a book in return and look bad tempered. It seemed strange to me. Why would they choose normally cheerful Margy for this?

At last we had a run-through. The cameras were in place, and four people lined up at the cashier's desk. At the head of the line was a tall, elderly man with a luxurious moustache, looking bored. Obviously, the action, what little there was would take place between the two of us. He handed me money and I gave him the book, putting on my best sour face. We did this three or four times. On the last take I was getting into being cranky, and I caught the elderly customer winking at me, or I thought he did. Finally, the director said he was satisfied. "We need you all to wait for a little while so we can check the film," he said. "Then we'll drive the SUV up here to the store and film it as well. Thank you, Ms. Pacsu. Thank you, Mr. Vonnegut."

At that moment a brand-new, bright orange Nissan Murano pulled up. I barely noticed it I was so awestruck. Mr. Vonnegut! *The* Kurt Vonnegut? The man who wrote *Cat's Cradle* and *Slaughterhouse-Five*? I turned to look at him. He shook his head, but I knew it *was* him. But why was Kurt Vonnegut in a commercial for a new SUV? Was this a dark satirical take on North American society, a sci-fi fantasy, a bitter anti-war insight into the human psyche? No. None of those things. It was just a commercial for a new car. I wished Gerry had told me who I'd be selling a book to.

There were a few chairs set up outside, and Vonnegut gestured toward them, saying, "Would you like to sit down here for a while?" He seemed kindly, but tired and a bit sad.

"When I drove up here this morning, I had no idea you would be my customer," I said.

"Well, unexpected events happen all the time," he replied. "So it goes."

I refrained from interviewing him and we started chatting. I explained I was from the States, but happy to be living in Canada now. He responded, "My daughter has just moved to Nova Scotia. She wants to become a Canadian. There is so much violence in New York nowadays."

At some point, the director popped his head out of his trailer to tell us the shot looked fine and then went back in. We continued our conversation. I talked a bit about my life in France and how I ended up in Toronto doing commercials. He spoke about living in New York and added he would soon be teaching at Smith College. A curious coincidence, I was a graduate class of 1960. He told me about another daughter who lived in Northampton, the charming small New England town where Smith College is located. He hoped she and her husband would look after him while he taught his two master classes in advanced writing. He was worried about his children but said it was his nature to be concerned about a bleak future. Eventually a black limousine pulled up, and he climbed in for the drive to the airport.

American author, Kurt Vonnegut, a quiet and somewhat sombre man, and I filmed a commercial for a new car. That sounds unlikely and it was certainly rather odd. We talked a lot during the long breaks in filming and when we parted he gave me this cartoon autograph.

I wished we'd had more time to talk. Before he left, he took out a publicity sheet for *Slaughterhouse-Five* on which he wrote, "For dear Margaret, supporting actress." He signed it with a caricature of himself – a fellow with a sharp pointy nose, a moustache, bushy hair – and added the date: Nov. 8, 2002. We had talked for a long time that afternoon, yet it never occurred to me to ask why he had agreed to do a commercial for a new SUV.

Chapter 19

Love recovered

After I left CBC in 1995, I no longer felt restricted by the demands of daily programs, so I was able to spend stretches of time with my mother in Princeton. She was in her early nineties, and although she was remarkably independent, she had problems with her eyesight. She still played the piano every day despite arthritis in her fingers and continued to learn new music by having the scores greatly enlarged and pasted on sheets of Bristol board propped up in front of her. On one visit, I discovered she was working on "Rumanische Weihnachtslieder I. Serie" (Romanian Christmas songs) by Béla Bartók.

But on April 10, 1998, my talented mother died quietly in her sleep at home aged ninety-three. Home-care nurses had taken care of her during the last few weeks, and my sister and nieces from Alaska and I took turns visiting Princeton to watch over her. I had just returned to Toronto when one of my nieces called at two o'clock in the morning to tell me the sad news. I have always regretted not being there to say goodbye and to help my niece look after the many details, the police report, the funeral arrangements. I was spared this anguish. You think you are prepared for the worst, but when death does come it is a devastating shock. My dear mother had left us.

The funeral took place at All Saints Episcopal Church in Princeton on April 16, a week after Easter Sunday. Flowers filled the church, most of them leftover from the previous week's Easter ceremony. The church service was beautiful, and the organist played Bach fugues and other music my mother loved. The Princeton musical community turned out in numbers, as did her former students, and many of my classmates from Miss Fine's School.

Bob gave a short address, reminding the congregation about her endearing qualities. He and my mother had a good relationship and shared an interest in politics. The two of them would have lengthy discussions, usually agreeing at the end. She held strong ideas about current affairs, politicians, and liberal views about women's rights with which Bob agreed. She had been an active socialist since she was a fifteen-year-old in 1918, demonstrating in the streets of Budapest. Except for two visits in the early thirties, from 1938 on, my parents had spent their lives in Princeton and did not visit Hungary again until 1962 and then went back several times. Anne and I encouraged them to take these trips home, as they had dreamed about doing so for years. We welcomed friends to the house after the funeral service, and the many stories about my mother they told us helped ease our sadness.

My mother was not only an outstanding pianist but had devoted her life to performing, recording, and instructing young people. Her contribution as musical accompanist for many years at Miss Fine's School allowed me to attend the school and had given her a certain notoriety. Not so well known was that she was one of Princeton's first female air spotters during the Second World War, something she was proud of. Her certificates for meritorious service in the Army Air Forces Fighter Command Ground Observer Corps attest to this.

We sat in her living room surrounded by her beloved objects, among them Attila's chest, our name for the large antique wooden box containing delicate bobbin-lace pieces made by a great aunt from Balatonendréd, a small Hungarian village known for this kind of hand work, and colorful red pillowcases embroidered with traditional flower designs. Mum had brought these pieces of Magyar art back from Budapest over the years. There were boxes piled upon boxes of my mother's collection of classical piano scores, many of them first editions. Several were Bartók's compositions and there was even an assortment of little-known mid-twentieth-century American composers. On the bookshelves, we found Hungarian literary masters and translations of foreign language works. One of my favorites is *War and Peace*, all thousand pages translated into Hungarian. Her prized possession, situated by the living room window where she could watch occasional deer passing by, was her faithful companion, the 1926 Steinway she bought second hand in 1932. She devoted as many hours playing that instrument as my father spent in his chemistry laboratory.

It took Anne and I many months to empty out our mother's house. We divided up the household belongings we each wanted to keep, always a difficult moment. Bob rented a well-used truck ("Sorry, it's the last one we have") to drive to Toronto. The Steinway was firmly tied in the back, along with a few pieces of furniture and dozens of boxes of music that the music department at the University of Toronto had promised to care for. Bob drove the heavily laden vehicle cautiously north up the Pennsylvania Turnpike, and I followed closely behind watching the van wallow like a boat in a storm. It's usually an eight-hour drive from Princeton to Toronto. This trip took much longer. It felt like the longest car trip of my life. As I followed along, I realized that I was probably leaving Princeton for the last time.

Some time later, I carried a stone in memory of my mother back to Budapest. By mistake I'd asked the stone carver to spell the month of her death in English instead of the Hungarian "Aprillus," but I think I was the only one who noticed. My sister Anne had already taken her ashes home which were buried in our grandfather's beloved garden in Mártonhegy looking down over Buda and the Danube. My father's ashes lie in the Pacsu family tomb across the river, in the large municipal Pest cemetery. My sister and I have fulfilled their abiding desire to be laid to rest in their beloved hometown.

What a marvelous adventure for them to settle in the New World. For my sister and I the adventure continues. For some sixty years, Anne has lived happily in Alaska, surrounded by the snow-covered mountains and wildlife she loves. Canada received me more than fifty years ago and gave me a sense of peace and belonging. Both of us have made a home in our chosen worlds but still have that dash of Magyar quirky unpredictability that leads to adventure.

What a long way I have traveled since that winter evening in the 1960s when I saw Chet in the smoky Blue Note nightclub in Paris. But in my imagination, I retrace my steps now, emerging from Saint-Philippe du Roule, the nearest Metro stop to the club. There's a faint murmur of traffic. The streetlights aren't on yet. It's the magical moment of twilight, which the French call *crepuscule*. I can hear a sweet, mellow sound in the distance, and I hurry toward it. You are standing in the shadows outside the Blue Note playing your trumpet. You're waiting for me. You look so young, the way I remember you on those early record covers. I am too. I sit down on a café chair to listen. You sing and play the songs I love to hear, "I Fall in Love Too Easily," "My Funny Valentine." The sun is below the horizon, but the sky is still rosy, pink. You come closer, this time folding me into your sweet sounds, your world-weary voice singing Kenny Dorham's "Fair Weather." I fade into the music. Not a cloud anywhere.

www.ingramcontent.com/pod-product-compliance
Lightning Source LLC
Chambersburg PA
CBHW050551160426
43199CB00015B/2618